THE COST OF COMMAND

EVERY FLAW HAS A ROLE. EVERY ROLE HAS A COST

DHARMESH MEHTA

© THE COST OF COMMAND
Dharmesh Mehta
1st Edition

Publication Date: April 2026
Price: ₹ 499 / $ 15
ISBN: 978-93-7164-403-7
Published by:
Adhyyan Books
Office No. 589,
Opposite Vivanta by Taj,
DDA SFS. Pocket-1, Dwarka,
Sec-22, New Delhi-110077
Website: http://adhyyanbooks.com
E-mail: contact@adhyyanbooks.com

Printed at: Repro Printers, Delhi

CONTENTS

PART I

ARCHETYPES IN ACTION

1

COMMAND UNDER FIRE

The heat slaps you in the face.

Walk onto the production floor of Apex Chemicals and you're hit by a wall of thick air that smells like burnt metal and sweet chemicals mixed together. It's forty-two degrees in here hot enough to make you sweat through your shirt in minutes. But that's what the reactors need. Those massive yellow tanks, each one tall as a two-story house, sit in rows along the eastern side of the building. Inside them, chemicals cook and bubble and turn into pharmaceutical compounds the building blocks for blood pressure medicine that ends up in seventy countries.

Eight hundred forty-seven families in Nadiad eat because of what happens in this building.

Ramesh Kumar works near Reactor 3. Not the Ramesh who's a manager this is Ramesh the operator, the guy who's been doing this job for sixteen years. Watch his hands move. Gloved, steady, touching valves and dials like a musician playing an instrument he knows by heart. One degree too hot and Rs. thirty lakhs of chemicals turn into garbage. Two degrees too cold and the batch take four extra hours to finish. They don't have four hours. The clients won't wait.

Ten feet away, Dinesh the floor supervisor stands with his clipboard pressed to his chest like armor. He doesn't trust the operators anymore. Three bad batches last month killed that trust.

"Ramesh! Temperature's going up on Reactor 3. You sleep over there?"

Ramesh doesn't look up. He's already seen it. Already fixing it. But Dinesh's voice carries across the whole floor, and other workers look over some worried, some embarrassed for Ramesh.

It didn't use to be like this.

Twenty-three years ago, Jayesh Thakkar built this place from nothing.

He believed India could make its own specialty chemicals. Didn't need to buy everything from foreign companies. He'd worked in German chemical plants for ten years, saved every rupee, and came back to Gujarat with blueprints rolled under his arm and dreams too big for most people to understand.

"We'll make what the world needs," he told his first ten workers in an empty warehouse. "And we'll make it better than anyone else."

For fifteen years, he was right.

Apex became the main supplier of pharmaceutical compounds to companies all over India, Southeast Asia, and parts of Europe. The factory ran three shifts every day. Workers brought their teenage sons in the factory to show them: "This is where you'll work someday. This is where your grandfather worked." Jayesh showed up every morning at six, rolled up his sleeves, and walked the floor asking people about their families, their problems, their ideas for making the things better.

Then eighteen months ago, Jayesh had a stroke.

A bad one. He lived, but barely. Now he sits in his office in Ahmedabad, half of his body not working right, words coming out slurred and wrong. His daughter reads him the quarterly reports. The doctors say he'll never walk these floors again.

So, leadership passed to the managers i.e. nine people, nine completely different ways of thinking, and they can't agree on anything.

That's when things started falling apart.

In the last six months, Apex lost two big clients. Both went to a Chinese company offering the same chemicals for eighteen percent less money. It's not about quality China's caught up. It's not about speed either. It's just price. And Apex can't match those prices without firing half the staff or working for zero profit.

The pharmaceutical business doesn't forgive mistakes. Contracts have penalty clauses. Regulations everywhere. And every client has backup suppliers waiting. One late shipment, one contaminated batch, one failed inspection, and they're gone. No warning. No second chances.

Apex is bleeding out.

Production dropped from 91% efficiency to 64% in four months. More batches are getting contaminated. Machines keep breaking down. Three senior chemists quit last quarter, all saying the same thing: "Management's a mess." Workers whisper about layoffs during tea breaks. Suppliers want faster payment now because everyone's heard the rumors Apex might not make it through the year.

Everyone's watching. Everyone's waiting to see if the ship goes down.

Arvind Desai stands on the observation deck above Reactor Hall - B. Fifteen feet up, separated from the noise by thick glass. From here he can see four production lines, eighteen reactors, sixty-three workers moving around like dancers in a routine they've done a thousand times.

He's been standing here for twenty minutes.

Just watching.

Arvind doesn't panic. He looks for patterns instead. And the pattern today is the same as last week and the week before a slow collapse dressed up to look like normal work.

Take Reactor 4. The cooling system's dying, but instead of shutting it down for real repairs, they're babying it along, hoping it survives until the quarter ends. Engineering says it needs two weeks off and twelve lakhs in new parts. Management says they can't afford two weeks or twelve lakhs.

So Reactor 4 runs at seventy percent, making less product, wearing itself out faster, buying time they're paying for in lost efficiency.

Arvind pulls out his leather notebook. Eight years old now, corners soft from being carried everywhere. Pages filled with his handwriting in neat columns: when machines break, how often workers call in sick, how many batches fail quality checks, when suppliers are late.

He writes: *Reactor 4 cooling about to die completely. Delaying repairs = bigger disaster. What costs more: fixing it now or dealing with total failure later?*

Down below, Dinesh is yelling again. This time at a young operator who questioned the valve sequence Dinesh ordered. The operator's right Arvind can see that from up here. Following Dinesh's sequence will create pressure problems in the line. But Dinesh hates being questioned, especially by someone young enough to be his son.

The operator gives up. Does it Dinesh's way.

Arvind clicks his pen twice. He always does that when something bothers him.

He writes: *Fix the culture or fixing the machines won't matter.*

His phone buzzes. Text from Meera Kapoor, the Operations Director:

Emergency meeting. 4 PM. Everyone needs to be there

Arvind checks his watch. Two hours.

He knows exactly how this meeting will go. He's sat through it a dozen times already, just with different dates on the calendar.

Meera will show them terrible numbers and demand they fix everything immediately. Rajesh will blame procurement and suppliers anyone but himself. Vikram will blame the workers, call them useless, say they should fire people. Kavita will talk about morale and keeping spirits up, which Vikram will laugh at. Ramesh the manager will crack some inappropriate joke to cut the tension, because jokes are easier than actual solutions. Dev will suggest automating everything, which will scare the older managers who don't trust technology. Suresh will sit there silent, gripping his pen so hard his knuckles go white, drowning in stress he can't talk about. And Priya will try to get everyone to work together, bless her heart, like that has any chance of working when nobody respects each other.

Same meeting. Different week. No decisions made. No progress.

Nine leaders going down together.

Arvind takes the metal stairs down to the floor. The noise hits him like a wave — reactors rumbling, steam hissing, metal banging on metal from the distillation units. The air's thick with sharp chemical smells and something sweet underneath that he's learned to identify just by breathing.

He walks slow, hands behind his back, watching everything.

Near Reactor 2, an operator named Prakash is manually adjusting feed rates because the automated system's broken. Each adjustment adds eleven seconds per batch. Do the math — an eight-hours shift, five days, four weeks the lost batches add up fast.

But Prakash hasn't reported the broken system.

Why? Because when you report problems, Dinesh blames you for them. Everyone's learned that lesson.

Arvind makes a mental note: *Feed system on Reactor 2 broken automation. Operator doing it by hand. Lost production = about six batches a month. What costs more: fixing it or losing six batches forever?*

Further down, near where they store solvents, a group of workers stands talking in low voices. Their body language looks tense shoulders hunched, heads close together. Arvind slows down, gets closer without being obvious about it.

"Third time this month they cut overtime," one says. Arvind recognizes him, Jayesh from Distillation Unit C. "How am I supposed to feed my family on just base pay?"

"They'll cut more than overtime next," someone else answers. "You seen the stock price? We're going down."

"My cousin works at the Vapi plant. Says they're hiring. May be we should start looking before this whole place shuts down."

They notice Arvind. Everyone stops talking. Eyes drop to the floor.

Arvind nods politely and keeps walking.

But the words stick with him.

We're going down.

They're not wrong.

Four o'clock. Conference room. Exactly what Arvind expected, but worse.

Meera stands at the front. Behind her, the screen shows graphs and numbers that all point in the wrong direction. Red arrows going down. Big words in capital letters: CRITICAL. UNSUSTAINABLE.

She's done trying to soften the message.

"Production efficiency dropped 42% across all reactor lines,"

Meera says, voice tight. "Contamination's up twenty-three percent. Customer complaints tripled. We lost MediCore Pharma and BioSynth Industries in the same quarter. If we don't turn this around in ninety days, corporate shuts us down and moves everything to Bangalore. We'll be the cautionary tale they tell at business schools."

Silence.

Then Vikram Rao leans back in his chair, arms crossed, face saying *I told you so*.

"Contamination's up because we hire idiots," Vikram says. "I've been saying it for months fire the bottom fifteen percent. Bring in people who actually care about quality. Pretty simple."

Kavita Sharma's head snaps toward him, eyes flashing. "Fire people? Vikram, morale's already terrible. You can't just"

"Morale?" Vikram laughs. Cold. Sharp. Mean. "Morale doesn't make pharmaceutical chemicals, Kavita. Competence does. You want to hold hands and sing songs while the place burns down? Go ahead. I'll be dealing with reality."

"I want to treat people like human beings, not machines you throw away."

"And I want results, not feelings."

Meera slams her hand on the table. The sound cracks through the room.

"Enough. Both of you. This isn't helping."

Rajesh Mehta sits in the middle where he can see everyone's faces. He's been on his phone this whole time. Now he puts it down slow, like the conversation finally got interesting enough for him.

"If I may," Rajesh says, voice smooth and reasonable in a way that makes Arvind suspicious, "the real problem isn't workers or morale. It's supply chain. Procurement's been buying cheap, low-quality materials to stay under budget. So we're building contamination into every batch from the start. Fix the inputs, fix the outputs. Basic economics."

Suresh Iyer, the procurement manager, looks like he's been slapped. His face goes pale. Jaw tight.

"We're buying within the exact budget limits *you* approved, Rajesh," Suresh says, voice shaking a little. "Don't rewrite history because it's convenient."

Rajesh smiles. Not a friendly smile. "I approved cost cuts. I didn't approve buying garbage from sketchy suppliers in Surat."

"You manipulative"

"Gentlemen," Priya Nair cuts in, voice calm but firm, like a teacher stopping a playground fight. "This isn't productive. We're not here to blame people. We're here to find solutions and work together."

"Solutions?" Dev Malhotra, youngest manager here at thirty-two, leans forward with that dangerous enthusiasm of someone who hasn't been crushed by bureaucracy yet. Eyes bright, almost feverish. "You want solutions? Automate Reactor Lines 3 and 4. Full digital monitoring. Cut manual work by forty percent, eliminate human mistakes, boost production by twenty-five percent. The technology exists. We're just scared to use it."

Vikram snorts. "Automate. Sure. Spend fifty lakhs we don't have on fancy computers that'll break just like everything else here."

"They won't break if we maintain them right and train people properly."

"And who maintains them? The same techs who can't keep our current equipment working?"

Dev's jaw tightens. "May be if we actually trained people instead of just yelling at them and threatening to fire them"

"May be if your generation understood that work isn't a motivational speech and everyone doesn't get a trophy"

"Enough!" Meera's voice cuts through. "I need action plans by Friday. All of you. Real plans with timelines and budgets. Not theories. Not blame. Solutions. Clear?"

Murmurs around the table.

Meera looks straight at Arvind, who's been quiet this whole time, slowly sipping water he hasn't really tasted.

"Arvind. You've been quiet. What do you think?"

Everyone turns to stare at him.

Arvind puts down his glass carefully. Takes a moment. Organizing his thoughts the way he organizes everything step by step, piece by piece.

What does he think?

He thinks they're all right and all wrong at the same time. Vikram's brutal but he's got a point buried under the cruelty — yes, some people really aren't doing their jobs and that matters. Kavita's empathy is necessary but it's not enough you can't motivate your way out of actual structural problems. Dev's innovation sounds good but it's reckless without proper planning and money they don't have. Rajesh is technically correct about supply chain problems but he's using that to hide his own failures. Suresh is drowning under impossible pressure nobody admits exists. Priya's collaboration sounds nice but it's powerless when nobody respects the process.

They're a textbook case of a failing organizations smart people, broken system, no shared vision, zero trust.

But he doesn't say any of that.

"I think," Arvind says slowly, picking each word carefully, "we need better data before we make decisions we can't undo. We're working with incomplete information and running on emotion. That's how you make catastrophic mistakes."

Vikram groans out loud. "Of course. More analysis. More data. More waiting. Rome's burning and Arvind's taking notes in his little book."

"Being impatient isn't strategy, Vikram. It's just panic with a deadline."

"And being cautious isn't leadership, Arvind. It's cowardice with fancy words."

The room goes dead silent.

Everyone holds their breath, waiting to see what Arvind does after getting called a coward to his face.

Arvind meets Vikram's glare without flinching. He figured out a long time ago that anger is just fear wearing a mask. Vikram's not really angry at him. Vikram's terrified the factory will collapse on his watch and prove he's the fraud he secretly thinks he is. The aggression is armor. The cruelty is protection.

Understanding that doesn't make it easier to hear, but it makes it easier to respond.

"I'd rather be slow and right," Arvind says quietly, "than fast and catastrophically wrong. History's full of leaders who confused urgency with wisdom."

Meera jumps in before Vikram can shoot back. "Action plans by Friday. End of discussion."

She shuts her laptop with a sharp snap.

Meeting over.

Later that evening, Arvind goes back to the observation deck. Second shift's running—now different workers, different rhythm, different light coming through the chemical haze. He stands at the glass watching reactors he understands way better than he understands people.

His phone buzzes. Message from a number he doesn't recognize:

You see the problems clearly. Why don't you fix them?

Arvind stares at it. Probably spam. Probably wrong number. Probably nothing.

He deletes it.

But it sticks with him. The question plants itself in his head and won't leave.

Why don't you fix them?

Because fixing means breaking things first. And Arvind doesn't break things. He watches. He analyzes. He writes patterns in leather notebooks. He waits for data to pile up, for certainty to appear, for the perfect moment when risk is low and success is guaranteed.

But what if certainty never comes?

What if the perfect moment is a fantasy, and patience is just paralysis with a better name?

What if Vikram's right?

He pulls out his notebook and writes: *When does patience stop being strategy and start being failure? When does wisdom become cowardice?*

Down on the floor, Reactor 4's cooling system alarm starts screaming. Workers run. Supervisors yell into radios. The system they've been nursing for weeks finally gave up.

Arvind watches from above rational, patient, observant, safe behind thick glass while the factory burns.

And for the first time in his career, he wonders if distance isn't wisdom.

Maybe it's just abandonment.

Maybe caution isn't smart.

Maybe it's just fear with better vocabulary.

The alarm keeps screaming. Red emergency lights flash across the reactor hall. Workers in yellow safety suits rush toward the crisis like they've practiced this a hundred times.

And Arvind stands in the shadows, clicking his pen twice, taking notes while his factory, Jayesh Thakkar's dream, eight hundred forty-seven families' paychecks, India's answer to imported chemicals goes down.

Watching.

Always watching.

Never quite ready to act.

2

HEARTS ON THE FLOOR

Kavita arrived at the plant at 5:47 AM, thirteen minutes before her shift officially started, because that's when the morning crew gathered near the tea stall outside Gate 2. Not for the tea—though Raju's chai was legitimately excellent—but because those thirteen minutes were when people were still human, before the reactors started and the roles hardened and everyone became operator or supervisor or manager instead of just Sunita or Prakash or Devi.

She paid for her own tea and for Malini's, who always arrived early but never had change. Small gesture. Malini smiled, tired but genuine, and that's what Kavita came for. That moment of connection. That recognition that beneath the safety vests and ID badges were beating hearts carrying mortgages and sick parents and children's school fees and dreams of something better.

"Your daughter's exam results came?" Kavita asked.

Malini's face lit up. "Ninety-two percent. Can you believe it? Ninety-two."

"I can believe it. She's brilliant. Just like her mother."

Malini laughed, the sound cutting through the pre-dawn chill. Others turned, curious. Kavita caught Dinesh watching from across the courtyard, his expression sour. He'd made it clear what he thought of "getting too close to the floor workers"—waste of time, blurring of boundaries, dangerous sentimentality.

Kavita made it a point to do it more.

The plant horn sounded. Six AM. The tea stall conversations ended mid-sentence as bodies moved toward the gates, the shift change choreography as precise as any reactor sequence inside. Kavita walked with them, not ahead, listening to the fragments of lives continuing from yesterday.

"...doctor said it's nothing serious, but the medicines..."

"...landlord raised rent again, I don't know how..."

"...my son wants to quit school, get a job, I told him over my dead body..."

These weren't just workers. They were people holding everything together with duct tape and determination, showing up every day to jobs that ground them down because someone depended on them to. And lately, Kavita watched that determination crumble, piece by piece, under the weight of production cuts and overtime cancellations and the constant, suffocating uncertainty.

She felt it. Every resignation, every exhausted face, every moment someone chose silence over speaking up because they'd learned that hope was dangerous here.

It was killing her.

Inside, the reactor floor was already chaos.

Reactor Hall 2 had three call-outs—illness, "family emergency," and one no-show. Dinesh was reassigning people, pulling operators from their familiar reactor assignments to cover gaps, which meant slower work and more mistakes and more of Dinesh's shouting, which meant more tension and more mistakes, a beautiful death spiral of dysfunction.

Kavita approached him carefully. "Dinesh, can we talk?"

"Busy."

"I can see. That's why we need to talk."

He finally looked at her, his face already red though the shift had barely started. "If this is another speech about morale—"

"This is a speech about production," Kavita said, keeping her voice level. "You're setting them up to fail. Anita doesn't know Reactor 2's systems. Putting her there without proper training—"

"She'll figure it out. They all figure it out or they leave. Natural selection."

"That's not how people work, Dinesh."

"That's exactly how people work. The strong survive. The weak wash out. You want to baby them, that's your business. I want production numbers."

"And how are those production numbers working out?"

The question landed like a slap. Dinesh's jaw worked silently for a moment before he stepped closer, voice dropping to something dangerous. "You don't get to question me on my floor, Kavita. I've been running operations here for twelve years. You've been in management for what, there? Don't confuse sympathy with competence."

"I'm not confusing anything. I'm watching good people burn out because you treat them like machines."

"They are machines. Expensive, unreliable, emotional machines that I have to keep running with insufficient resources and impossible targets while people like you make it harder by filling their heads with ideas that they matter."

Kavita felt something cold settle in her chest. "They do matter."

"Then where are they?" Dinesh swept his arm across the floor. "Three call-outs today. Five yesterday. Eight last week. If they mattered, they'd show up."

"Maybe they'd show up if there was something worth showing up for."

Dinesh smiled, but there was no warmth in it. "You really believe that, don't you? You think if we just care enough, sing enough kumbaya, everyone'll hold hands and we'll magically hit our targets. That's not reality, Kavita. Reality is that this plant is dying, and your feelings can't save it."

He walked away before she could respond.

Kavita stood there, heart pounding, hands shaking slightly. Around her, the reactors roared their indifference. Operators moved like ghosts, heads down, going through motions. No one met her eyes.

She wanted to scream. She wanted to gather everyone and tell them they deserved better. She wanted to march into Meera's office and demand they fire Dinesh, restructure supervision, invest in people instead of just equipment.

But she'd tried that. Multiple times. And the response was always the same: *We need results, not therapy.*

As if the two were separate. As if you could extract performance from broken people indefinitely.

By ten AM, Reactor 2 had completed only 3 batches with 847 kg output. Target was 5 batches yielding 1,200 kg by noon.

Kavita watched the gap widen and felt it like a physical thing, a weight pressing down on her shoulders. Because the gap meant failed targets, which meant more pressure from corporate, which meant more cuts, which meant more suffering, which meant more resignations, which meant fewer people to carry the load, which meant more pressure, more cuts, more suffering.

The spiral only went one direction.

She walked the floor, stopping at each reactor control station, asking questions, listening. This was her superpower, according to Priya, this ability to see people. But lately it felt less like a superpower and more like a curse, because seeing meant feeling, and feeling meant carrying everyone's pain in addition to her own.

At Reactor 2's control panel, she found Anita struggling with the unfamiliar parameters, her adjustments hesitant, uncertain. Two batches had already been flagged for quality review that morning.

"Hey," Kavita said softly. "First time operating Reactor 2?"

Anita nodded, not looking up. "I'm sorry. I'm trying, I just—the temperature protocols are different, and I keep—"

"It's not your fault. You shouldn't be here without proper training." Kavita glanced around, then reached for the control interface. "Look, the reactor pressure needs to be maintained in this range—see? And the reagent feed rate is controlled by this valve system, not the manual bypass. The interface is terrible, I know, but that's what we're working with."

She walked Anita through three batch cycles, narrating each step, correcting gently, praising the adjustments. Within fifteen minutes, Anita's movements smoothed. The batch failure rate dropped.

"You're doing great," Kavita said. "Just remember—pressure first, then feed rate, then temperature compensation. You've got this."

Anita looked at her, really looked at her, and something in that gaze made Kavita's throat tight. Gratitude, yes. But also,something sadder. Surprise. As if basic decency was so rare here that it registered as extraordinary.

"Thank you, ma'am," Anita said quietly.

"Kavita. Just Kavita."

She moved to the next reactor, then the next, troubleshooting, encouraging, adjusting. At Reactor 5's monitoring station, she found Ramesh—the operator, not the manager—sitting motionless, staring at his gauges.

"Ramesh? You okay?"

He blinked, coming back from wherever his mind had gone. "Yeah. Fine."

"You don't look fine."

"Just tired, ma'am. Didn't sleep well."

Kavita pulled up a stool, ignoring the voice in her head that sounded suspiciously like Dinesh telling her she was wasting time. "What's going on?"

Ramesh hesitated, then the words spilled out. "My father needs surgery. Hip replacement. The government hospital has a six-month wait list. Private hospital wants three lakhs. I've been working doubles, but with the overtime cuts..." He trailed off, shaking his head. "It's fine. We'll figure it out."

"Have you talked to HR about the medical assistance program?"

"I tried. They said the program's suspended. Budget constraints."

Of course it was. Cut the programs people needed most, keep the executive bonuses flowing. The casual cruelty of it made Kavita want to break something.

"Let me talk to them," she said. "And Ramesh? Take your breaks. I know you've been skipping lunch. You can't pour from an empty cup."

He nodded, but they both knew he'd keep skipping lunch because every saved rupee mattered when your father needed surgery and the system didn't care.

Kavita stood, her chest aching. How many stories like this lived in this building? How many silent struggles, quiet desperation, dreams deferred indefinitely? And what good did it do for her to feel it all if she couldn't fix any of it?

The afternoon production meeting was brutal.

Meera stood at the whiteboard, marking the morning's numbers in red. Reactor 2: sixty-eight percent yield efficiency. Reactor 4: fifty-nine percent. Overall facility performance: seventy-one percent.

"Unacceptable," Meera said flatly. "Completely unacceptable."

Vikram leaned back in his chair. "I've been saying—"

"I know what you've been saying, Vikram. Fire everyone, start over. Very constructive."

"More constructive than whatever Kavita's doing. How many heart-to-hearts did we have today, Kavita? How many feelings did we validate? And what did it get us? Sixty-eight percent."

Kavita felt the room's attention shift to her. She met Vikram's eyes, refusing to look away. "I got us operators who didn't walk out mid-shift. I got us people who came back after lunch instead of just disappearing. You want to know what your approach gets us? Eight resignations in two weeks. People would rather be unemployed than work under you."

"Good. Weak links removing themselves."

"They weren't weak. They were broken. By us. By this place. By people like you who think cruelty is management."

Vikram's smile was sharp. "And people like you think therapy is production strategy. Tell me, Kavita—when the plant closes, when we're all unemployed, will it comfort you that people liked you? That you were nice?"

The words hit harder than they should have because Kavita had been asking herself the same question. She was nice. She did care. She spent hours listening, encouraging, supporting. And the numbers still fell. The plant still spiraled. The suffering still mounted.

Was Vikram right? Was compassion just self-indulgence when results were all that mattered?

"Being nice," Kavita said slowly, "isn't weakness, Vikram. It's the only thing keeping this place from complete collapse. You break people and wonder why they don't perform. I try to hold them together. Maybe if you tried treating humans like humans instead of disposable tools—"

"We'd still be failing, but everyone would feel better about it. Fantastic strategy."

Meera held up a hand. "Enough. Both approaches are failing. We need something different."

"We need accountability," Dinesh muttered.

"We need support," Kavita shot back.

Dev spoke up. "We need automation—"

"We need to stop having the same useless arguments," Rajesh interrupted smoothly. "The problem isn't management style. The problem is resource allocation, supply chain, strategic positioning—"

The meeting dissolved into the usual chaos. Kavita stopped listening. She'd heard it all before. Everyone had the answer. No one could agree. Meanwhile, real people suffered in the gap between theory and action.

That evening, Kavita found herself back at the tea stall, long after her shift ended. The plant lights blazed behind her, second shift in full swing. She should go home. She should rest. She should stop carrying everyone's pain like it was hers to bear.

But Anita was probably still struggling at Reactor 2. And Ramesh was worrying about his father. And tomorrow three more people might call out because they'd lost hope that anything would change.

Her phone buzzed. A message from Priya: *You okay? You seemed upset earlier.*

Kavita typed back: *Just tired.*

The truth was more complicated. She wasn't just tired. She was exhausted by caring in a place that punished caring. She was drowning in empathy that couldn't translate to results. She was starting to wonder if Vikram and Dinesh and even Arvind with his endless patience were right—that emotion was a liability, that hearts had no place on reactor floors, that trying to love people into performance was naive at best and destructive at worst.

But then she thought of Anita's grateful smile. Ramesh's tentative trust. Malini's daughter's exam results. These moments mattered. They had to matter.

Even if the spreadsheets said otherwise.

Kavita finished her tea, cold now, and walked back through the gates. Tomorrow she'd try again. She'd listen again. She'd care again. Because if she stopped caring, what was left? Just reactors and numbers and the slow death of everything that made them human.

The plant could take a lot from them.

But it couldn't take that.

Not yet.

3

THE EQUATION OF INFLUENCE

Rajesh Mehta learned three things in his first week at Apex Chemicals, back when he was just a junior manager nobody paid attention to.

One: The person who controls information controls the room.

Two: Every person has a weakness—you just need to find it and file it away for later.

Three: Never let them see you sweat. Ever.

Twelve years later, those three rules had carried him from junior manager to Senior VP of Supply Chain and Strategic Partnerships. Not bad for someone who started out making tea runs and formatting PowerPoint slides nobody read.

He arrived at the plant at 8:47 AM, exactly thirteen minutes late for the morning operations briefing. Not an accident. Walking in late meant everyone was already seated, which meant all eyes turned to you when you entered. Small thing, but Rajesh had built his entire career on small things that added up to power.

"Sorry, everyone," he said, sliding into his seat with a smile that didn't quite reach his eyes. "Corporate had me on a call. You know how it is."

He didn't have a call. He'd been in his car in the parking lot, scrolling through WhatsApp messages and emails, gathering intelligence. But *corporate had me on a call* was a useful phrase. It reminded everyone that he had access they didn't, relationships that went above their heads, a lifeline to the people who actually made decisions.

Meera gave him a look that said she knew exactly what he was doing, but she continued with her presentation anyway. Production numbers. Quality metrics. The usual disaster painted in red bars on a graph.

Rajesh half-listened while appearing completely engaged—another skill he'd mastered. Nod at the right moments. Furrow his brow during the concerning parts. Take notes that were actually just doodles disguised as important observations.

His phone buzzed silently on his lap. A message from Karan Deshmukh, a mid-level manager in Quality Control.

Boss, got that info you asked about. Can we meet?

Rajesh typed back without looking at his phone, fingers moving purely by muscle memory.

My office. 11:30.

Then he put the phone away and refocused on the meeting just as Arvind started talking about data collection timelines and the need for systematic analysis before making major decisions.

Arvind was exhausting. Smart, sure. Observant, absolutely. But so painfully slow. The kind of person who'd research dinner options for three hours and still end up eating dal-chawal because nothing else met his criteria.

"Arvind," Rajesh said, leaning forward with practiced concern, "I appreciate the thoroughness. I really do. But we're bleeding out here. Every day we spend collecting perfect data is another day we lose market share to competitors who are moving faster than us."

Arvind's jaw tightened almost imperceptibly. "Moving fast without understanding the problem is how you make it worse."

"And moving slow with perfect understanding is how you go extinct while understanding exactly why."

A few people around the table shifted uncomfortably. Meera jumped in before it could escalate.

"Both perspectives are valid. Let's focus on—"

"Actually," Rajesh interrupted smoothly, "while we're all here, I should mention something. I've been in discussions with a potential new supplier in Pune. They can cut our raw material costs by twenty-two percent and maintain quality standards. I'm meeting with them next week to finalize terms."

The room went quiet.

Suresh, the procurement manager, looked like he'd been slapped. "What? I'm procurement. Why wasn't I—"

"You've been under a lot of stress lately, Suresh," Rajesh said gently, almost sympathetically. "I didn't want to add to your plate. Thought I'd handle the preliminary discussions and loop you in once we had something concrete."

It sounded reasonable. It sounded like he was being considerate.

It was neither.

What it actually was: Rajesh going around Suresh because Suresh asked too many questions and moved too slowly and didn't understand that sometimes you had to make deals happen before the bureaucracy killed them. If this supplier worked out, Rajesh would get credit for saving the company money. If it failed, well, he'd looped in Suresh eventually, hadn't he? Shared responsibility. Diffused blame.

Suresh opened his mouth, then closed it. His hands were shaking slightly. He looked at Meera, silently asking for support.

Meera's expression was unreadable. "We'll discuss the supplier chain of command separately. Right now, let's—"

"Of course," Rajesh said easily. "Just thought the team should know we're exploring options. That's what strategic partnerships means, right? Being strategic."

He smiled.

The meeting continued, but the damage was done. Suresh sat there looking smaller, deflated. Rajesh had just publicly undercut him while making it sound like a favor, and everyone in the room knew it.

Everyone except maybe Ramesh, the manager version, who was barely paying attention anyway, probably rehearsing whatever joke he'd crack later to defuse the tension.

After the meeting broke up, Rajesh made his way back to his office—corner location, third floor, windows overlooking the reactor halls. He'd specifically requested this office when they reorganized two years ago. Not the biggest office, but the positioning mattered. You could see who was coming and going. Who was meeting with whom. Who was avoiding whom.

Information. Control.

At 11:30 exactly, Karan knocked on the door.

"Come in. Close it behind you."

Karan was young, ambitious, and deeply insecure about his position—which made him perfect for what Rajesh needed. He'd cultivated Karan carefully over the past eight months. Small favors. Casual mentions of Karan's good work in front of senior management. An invitation to a dinner meeting with suppliers where Karan got to feel important.

All of it calculated. All of it building to moments like this.

"What did you find?" Rajesh asked, not bothering with pleasantries.

Karan pulled out his phone, scrolling through photos. "You were right. Three batches from last month—lots 4782, 4791, and 4805—all had quality flags that were overridden by supervisors. Not reported up the chain. Just… ignored."

"Supervisors — more than one?"

"Dinesh signed off on two of them. Prakash Reddy on the third."

Rajesh leaned back in his chair, fingers steepled. Interesting. Very interesting.

Dinesh was already on thin ice after the incident last quarter where his aggressive management style got mentioned in an anonymous HR complaint. And Prakash, while technically competent, had a reputation for cutting corners when targets got tight.

"Send me those photos," Rajesh said. "Don't share them with anyone else. And Karan? Good work. I won't forget this."

Karan practically glowed. "Of course, boss. Anything you need."

After Karan left, Rajesh sat there thinking.

He had leverage now. Information that could be used or not used, depending on what the situation required. If Dinesh became a problem—which, given his combative nature, was only a matter of time—Rajesh could surface these quality overrides. Raise concerns about supervisor accountability. Position himself as the person who cared about standards while others looked the other way.

But if he needed Dinesh compliant, cooperative, willing to support Rajesh's initiatives? Well, then this information stayed private. A favor, unspoken but understood. *I could have buried you, but I didn't. Remember that.*

This was the game. And Rajesh was very, very good at it.

His phone rang. Unknown number. Rajesh almost didn't answer —he screened calls religiously—but something made him pick up.

"Rajesh Mehta."

"Mr. Mehta, this is Anand Kumar from MediCore Pharma."

Rajesh sat up straighter. MediCore was one of the major clients they'd lost last quarter. Corporate was still furious about it.

"Mr. Kumar. What a surprise. How can I help you?"

"I wanted to reach out directly, off the record. We're... reconsidering some of our supplier relationships. The Chinese firm we switched to has had quality issues. Three failed batches in two months."

Rajesh's mind started racing, but his voice stayed calm. "I'm sorry to hear that. Quality problems can be very costly."

"Indeed. Look, if Apex could match pricing—say, within eight percent of current rates—and guarantee delivery timelines, we'd be willing to discuss bringing some contracts back. But this would need to happen quickly. And quietly. We can't have our current supplier knowing we're shopping around until terms are finalized."

Eight percent. That was a big gap. Their current cost structure couldn't absorb that without serious cuts somewhere—labor, materials, overhead, something had to give.

But getting MediCore back would be enormous. Corporate would throw a parade. Rajesh would be the hero who saved a key account.

"I think we can make that work," Rajesh said smoothly. "Give me a week to run the numbers and put together a proposal. Can we meet next Thursday? Somewhere neutral—maybe that café in Anand?"

"Thursday works. 3 PM."

"Perfect. And Mr. Kumar? This stays between us for now."

"Understood."

The call ended.

Rajesh sat there, mind spinning through possibilities. Eight percent cost reduction. How?

Cheaper raw materials—which meant going even lower quality than what Suresh was already being blamed for. Or automation, Dev's obsession, which would mean layoffs and union problems. Or renegotiating labor contracts, cutting benefits, eliminating overtime—political suicide that would have workers rioting.

Or… all of the above, but positioned cleverly. Blame it on corporate mandates. Make it sound inevitable, like forces beyond anyone's control. Get people fighting with each other instead of unified against management.

His door opened without knocking. Vikram walked in like he owned the place.

"We need to talk," Vikram said, closing the door hard enough that it was almost a slam.

Rajesh gestured to the chair across from his desk, unfazed. "By all means."

Vikram sat, arms crossed, jaw tight. "You went around Suresh this morning. In front of everyone."

"I initiated supplier discussions that fall under strategic partnerships, which is my domain."

"Bullshit. You undermined him publicly because that's what you do. You play people against each other."

Rajesh smiled. Not warmly. "And you don't?"

"I'm direct. I tell people they're failing because they are. You're indirect. You knife people while smiling and calling it teamwork."

"Is there a point to this visit, Vikram?"

"Yeah. The point is you're making this situation worse. We're supposed to be leadership, but you treat it like a chess game where everyone else is a piece you move around."

"And you treat it like a battlefield where everyone's an enemy you need to crush. At least my approach doesn't drive people to quit."

Vikram leaned forward, voice dropping to something dangerous. "You think you're clever. You think your little political games make you valuable. But when this place goes down—and it will go down if we don't fix things fast—your networking and your favors and your manipulation won't mean shit. You'll just be another executive with a fancy title on a dead company's org chart."

"Is that a threat?"

"It's reality. You're too busy protecting yourself to actually lead."

"And you're too busy destroying people to build anything."

They stared at each other across the desk, two completely different types of toxicity meeting in the middle.

Finally, Vikram stood. "Stay out of my way, Rajesh."

"Likewise."

After Vikram left, Rajesh sat there for a long moment.

The accusation stung more than he wanted to admit. Not because it wasn't true—it absolutely was true—but because it was said out loud. Named. Made real.

He did play chess with people. He did manipulate situations to his advantage. He'd built an entire career on knowing where the bodies were buried, who owed whom favors, how to position himself as indispensable while making others look dispensable.

And it worked. It got him promoted. It got him respect, or at least the appearance of it. It kept him safe when others were fired or demoted or sidelined.

But.

Vikram wasn't entirely wrong. The plant was dying, and Rajesh's usual tactics weren't stopping it. You couldn't politic your way out of broken reactors and contaminated batches and clients leaving for better offers.

At some point, someone actually had to fix things.

But that someone didn't have to be him, did it?

His role was strategic partnerships. Relationships. Positioning. Let the operators fix the technical problems. Let Meera handle operations. Let Arvind analyze everything to death. Rajesh's job was to make sure that when the dust settled, he was still standing.

That's what mattered. Survival.

Later that afternoon, Rajesh ran into Priya near the cafeteria.

She was talking to a group of floor workers—actually talking, not just pretending to listen while thinking about something else. Rajesh waited until the conversation ended and the workers dispersed.

"Priya. Got a minute?"

She turned, and her expression was careful. Priya was smart. She saw through people, including him.

"What do you need, Rajesh?"

"Need? Can't I just want to chat with a colleague?"

"You don't chat. You gather intelligence and position pieces. So what is it?"

He laughed, genuine for once. "Fair. Okay. I wanted to talk about Suresh."

"What about him?"

"He's drowning. You see it. I see it. Everyone sees it. And it's affecting his department, which affects procurement, which affects production. We need to address it."

"By 'address it,' you mean replace him."

"I mean help him. Or move him to a role that's less pressure. He's a good guy, Priya. But he's in over his head."

Priya studied him for a long moment. "Why do you care?"

"Because we're a team. When one person fails, we all—"

"Rajesh. Please. Don't insult my intelligence with corporate speak."

He stopped. Recalibrated.

"Fine. Honest answer? Suresh being overwhelmed makes my job harder. His delayed decisions slow down supplier relationships, which makes me look bad when deals fall through. So yes, I have selfish reasons for wanting him in a different role. But that doesn't mean I'm wrong about him needing help."

Priya nodded slowly. "At least that's honest."

"Will you talk to Meera? She trusts you. If it comes from you, it won't look like I'm undermining him."

"Which is exactly why you want me to do it."

"Which is exactly why it might actually work."

Priya sighed. "I'll think about it. But Rajesh? Eventually, you're going to have to decide whether you want to be the person who wins office politics or the person who actually saves this place. You can't be both."

She walked away before he could respond.

Rajesh stood there, her words echoing in his head.

You can't be both.

But what if saving the place meant losing the game? What if doing the right thing meant exposing himself, making himself vulnerable, trusting people who might turn on him the moment it became convenient?

He'd spent twelve years learning not to do that. Twelve years building walls, calculating angles, protecting himself first. You didn't survive corporate life by being noble. You survived by being smart, by being two steps ahead, by making sure other people took the fall when things went wrong.

That evening, driving home through Nadiad's chaotic traffic, Rajesh got another message. This time from his wife.

Your daughter's parent-teacher conference is tomorrow. 4 PM. You promised you'd be there.

Shit. He'd forgotten. Again.

He typed back: **Something came up at work. Can you handle it?**

Three dots appeared, then disappeared. Then appeared again.

You always have something at work. She asked if you were coming. What should I tell her?

Rajesh stared at the message, stuck at a red light, auto-rickshaws honking around him.

What should she tell their daughter? That Daddy was too busy playing political games to show up for the people who actually loved him? That strategic partnerships mattered more than parent-teacher conferences? That he was very good at managing relationships with people who could advance his career and very bad at managing relationships with people who just wanted him present?

He typed: **I'll be there. Promise.**

But even as he sent it, he was already thinking about the meeting with MediCore on Thursday, the supplier negotiations that needed finalization, the quarterly review where he needed to present wins to corporate to justify his position.

The light turned green. Rajesh drove forward, phone buzzing with new messages, his mind already three moves ahead.

Always calculating. Always positioning. Always protecting.

Never quite there.

Back at the plant, in his office that he'd locked when he left, a sticky note was attached to his computer monitor. He hadn't noticed it when he left, and he wouldn't see it until tomorrow morning.

It was in handwriting he wouldn't recognize, and it said only:

They know what you're doing. Everyone knows. The question is—do you?

4

THE FOOL'S GAMBIT

Ramesh Patel—the manager, not the operator—discovered his superpower in ninth standard when his father died.

The day after the funeral, his mother was crying in the kitchen, trying to cook lunch with shaking hands. His younger sister wouldn't come out of her room. The house felt like it was suffocating under the weight of grief nobody knew how to carry.

So Ramesh told a joke.

A stupid joke about their neighbor's goat that had eaten someone's newspaper. It wasn't even that funny. But his mother laughed—just for a second, this small hiccup of sound that broke through the crying. And his sister came out of her room to hear what the noise was about.

That's when Ramesh learned: humor doesn't fix things, but it makes them bearable. It creates space to breathe when everything's crushing you.

Twenty-three years later, he'd turned that survival mechanism into a management style. Some people called it unprofessional. Others called it inappropriate. Ramesh called it the only reason half the people in this building still smiled when the shift bell rang.

He showed up at the plant at 9:15 AM wearing a shirt with a small coffee stain on the collar that he'd tried and failed to hide. His daughter had spilled milk at breakfast, his car had made a concerning grinding noise the entire drive, and his credit card payment was due tomorrow with funds he didn't quite have yet.

But none of that showed on his face.

"Morning, morning!" he called out, walking through the main corridor with the energy of someone who'd had eight hours of sleep instead of four and a half. "Who's ready for another thrilling day of chemical excellence and workplace dysfunction?"

A few people smiled despite themselves. Others rolled their eyes—the usual split.

Near the time-clock station, he found a cluster of operators looking at a notice someone had posted on the board:

MANDATORY OVERTIME CANCELLED UNTIL FURTHER NOTICE

The mood was dark. These weren't just numbers on a policy memo—this was rent money, school fees, the difference between getting by and not getting by.

"They're killing us slowly," someone muttered. "First overtime, next it'll be base pay cuts."

"Or layoffs," another voice added.

Ramesh squeezed into the group, reading the notice like it was news to him even though he'd been in the meeting where it was decided. Actually, he'd argued against it. Lost, obviously, but he'd tried.

"Well," Ramesh said loudly, "look at the bright side."

Everyone turned to stare at him.

"The bright side?" Jayesh from Distillation Unit C looked at him like he'd lost his mind. "What bright side?"

"Now you'll actually have time to go home and see what your families look like. I've been here so long I forgot I had a wife. Went home last month, strange woman opened the door. Turns out I married her twelve years ago. Wild."

A couple of people snorted. Not quite laughs, but close enough.

"Easy for you to joke," Jayesh said, but his voice had lost some of its edge. "You're not the one trying to figure out how to pay rent with twenty percent less income."

"You're right. I'm trying to figure out how to pay rent with a thirty percent less income and a daughter who wants dance lessons that cost more than my kidney's probably worth on the black market. We're all broke together. It's very democratic."

This time a few actual laughs.

"Dance lessons?" Malini asked. "Your daughter's doing Bharatanatyam?"

"Hip-hop. Apparently, classical dance is 'for old people,' which is what she said right before asking me—an old person—to pay for it. The irony was not lost on me even if the money was."

More laughter. The group's body language shifted slightly—shoulders less hunched, expressions less rigid.

Ramesh knew he couldn't fix their financial stress. Couldn't magically restore overtime or raise their salaries or make the company less of a sinking ship. But he could give them thirty seconds where the weight felt lighter. Where they remembered they were people, not just workers drowning in circumstances beyond their control.

"Alright, back to making chemicals that save lives or something equally noble," Ramesh said, waving them off. "And remember—we're not just employees, we're a family. A deeply dysfunctional family that's probably getting divorced, but still."

They dispersed, most of them smiling at least a little bit.

Ramesh's own smile dropped the second they weren't looking.

The management meeting started at 10:30, and it was exactly as painful as he'd expected.

Meera was presenting updated financial projections, each slide worse than the last. Red numbers everywhere. Downward trends that looked like they'd been designed to induce panic.

"We're looking at a twenty-eight percent revenue shortfall this quarter," Meera said, her voice carrying that special kind of exhaustion that came from delivering bad news over and over again. "If this trajectory continues, corporate is projecting full operational shutdown by Q3."

Silence around the table. The heavy kind, where everyone's thinking the same thing but nobody wants to say it out loud.

Finally, Vikram spoke up. "Then we make cuts. Aggressive cuts. Now."

"We've already cut overtime," Suresh said weakly.

"I'm not talking about overtime. I'm talking about people. Thirty percent workforce reduction, start with the bottom performers, and—"

"Fire three hundred people?" Kavita's voice rose. "Vikram, that's not a solution, that's a massacre."

"It's called business, Kavita. Maybe you've heard of it."

"It's called cruelty disguised as—"

Ramesh cleared his throat loudly. Everyone turned to look at him.

"Sorry, sorry," he said, waving his hand. "I was just wondering—if we fire thirty percent of the workforce, do we get to choose which thirty percent of our own bodies to cut off? Because I'm thinking I could lose a foot. Don't use it much anyway. Very overrated, feet."

A beat of silence.

Then Priya cracked, letting out a small laugh she tried to hide behind her hand.

"This isn't funny, Ramesh," Vikram said coldly.

"Nothing about this is funny. That's why I'm making jokes. Someone has to, or we're all going to jump off the reactor observation deck together. Which, by the way, I call dibs on going first. I want the good spot with the view."

"Could we focus, please?" Meera's voice cut through, but there was something in her expression—not quite a smile, but not quite as rigid as before.

The meeting continued, cycling through the same arguments they'd been having for months. Cut costs. Don't cut costs. Fire people. Don't fire people. Innovate. No, that's too expensive. Around and around, a carousel of dysfunction that never actually moved forward.

Ramesh watched it all with the expression of someone paying attention while his mind was actually calculating whether he could afford his car payment this month if he skipped lunch for the next three weeks.

At one point, Arvind started talking about long-term strategic planning, and Rajesh interrupted to talk about supplier negotiations, and then Vikram interrupted both of them to call everyone idiots, and Kavita jumped in to defend people's dignity, and Dev tried to bring it back to automation, and Suresh just sat there looking like he was aging in real-time.

Ramesh waited for a gap in the chaos.

"Can I make a suggestion?" he asked.

Everyone turned to him, expressions ranging from curious to irritated.

"What if," Ramesh said slowly, "and hear me out here—what if we tried not running this place like a competition to see who can make the worst decision fastest?"

Vikram snorted. "Brilliant insight, Ramesh. Very helpful."

"I'm serious. Look at us. We're nine people who can't agree on anything, sitting around a table coming up with elaborate plans to fail in slightly different ways. Meanwhile, the actual people doing actual work downstairs are watching their leaders have a collective meltdown and wondering if they should update their resumes."

"So what's your solution?" Rajesh asked, his voice carrying that particular tone that meant he was about to dismiss whatever came next.

"I don't have one. That's the point. None of us do. Not really. Arvind wants to study the problem for six months, Vikram wants to burn everything down, Kavita wants to hug it out, Dev wants to replace humans with robots—"

"That's not what I—"

"—and Rajesh wants to make deals that sound good in meetings but nobody actually understands. We're all just guessing and pretending we're not."

The room went very quiet.

Meera leaned forward. "What's your point, Ramesh?"

"My point is maybe we should stop pretending we have answers and start admitting we're scared shitless and have no idea what we're doing. At least then we'd be honest."

"Honesty doesn't pay the bills," Vikram said.

"Neither does whatever we're doing now."

Nobody had a response to that.

The meeting ended without any decisions made, which was becoming a theme. People filed out, most of them avoiding eye contact with each other.

Ramesh hung back, gathering his papers slowly, watching Meera shut down her laptop with the kind of forceful clicking that suggested she was imagining it was someone's head.

"That was fun," Ramesh said. "We should do it again never."

Meera looked at him, and for just a second, her professional mask slipped. She looked tired. Really tired. The kind of tired that sleep didn't fix.

"Do you ever take anything seriously, Ramesh?"

"All the time. I'm just also aware that taking things seriously and pretending you have control are different things. One's useful. The other's delusion."

"Which one am I doing?"

"Honestly? Both. But at least you're trying. That's more than most of us."

She studied him for a moment. "You know, people think you're just the office clown."

"I know. I encourage it. Lower expectations mean fewer disappointments."

"But you're not, are you? Just a clown."

Ramesh picked up his papers, tapping them against the table to straighten them even though they were already straight. "We're all playing roles, Meera. Mine just happens to be the one that keeps people from crying in the bathroom. Someone's got to do it."

He left before she could ask any follow-up questions he didn't want to answer.

The afternoon shift was when things usually fell apart, and today was no exception.

Ramesh was doing his walkthrough of the production floor when he heard shouting near Reactor 6. He walked over to find Dinesh in the middle of dressing down a young operator named Pradeep.

"—completely unacceptable! You think you can just ignore protocol because you feel like it?"

Pradeep stood there, face red, fists clenched at his sides. "I didn't ignore protocol, sir. The valve sequence you ordered would have created a pressure spike in the—"

"Are you arguing with me?"

"I'm trying to explain—"

"You're trying to make excuses for incompetence. This is why production numbers are in the toilet. People like you who think they know better than—"

"Hey, Dinesh!" Ramesh's voice cut through, cheerful and loud. "Got a second?"

Dinesh turned, his expression making it very clear he did not, in fact, have a second.

"I'm in the middle of something, Ramesh."

"I can see that. Public humiliation, one of the classics. Very old school. I respect it." He turned to Pradeep. "You okay?"

Pradeep nodded, not trusting his voice.

"Cool. Go take your break. I'll handle this."

After Pradeep left, Dinesh rounded on Ramesh. "What the hell do you think you're doing? You just undermined me in front of—"

"In front of nobody. He left. It's just us now. And I'm going to tell you something that's going to make you very angry, but I need you to hear it anyway."

Dinesh crossed his arms. "I'm listening."

"You're breaking people. On purpose. And I get it—you're under pressure, we're all under pressure, the entire building is basically a pressure cooker at this point. But taking it out on kids who are just trying to do their jobs? That's not management. That's just cruelty with a clipboard."

"That 'kid' almost caused a batch failure because he—"

"Because he questioned your valve sequence, which, between you and me, was probably wrong. I saw the setup. He was right to question it."

Dinesh's face went a dangerous shade of red. "You're telling me how to do my job now?"

"I'm telling you that if you keep treating people like this, you won't have anyone left to supervise. Three resignations last week. Five the week before. And they're not leaving because the work is hard. They're leaving because you are."

For a second, Ramesh thought Dinesh might actually hit him. His entire body was rigid, jaw working silently.

Then, quietly, Dinesh said: "Get out of my sight."

"Dinesh—"

"GET OUT."

Ramesh left.

He found Pradeep in the break room, sitting alone, staring at nothing.

"You okay?" Ramesh asked, sitting down across from him.

Pradeep shrugged. "I'm used to it."

"You shouldn't have to be."

"Doesn't matter what I should or shouldn't have to be. It's how it is."

Ramesh wanted to argue, but what would he say? That things would get better? That standing up to people like Dinesh would change anything? That this place valued fairness and dignity?

All lies. Well-meaning lies, maybe, but lies nonetheless.

"Look," Ramesh said finally. "I can't fix Dinesh. I can't fix this place. But I can tell you that what happened just now? That wasn't about you. That was about him being scared and angry and taking it out on whoever's closest. You did nothing wrong."

"Doesn't change anything."

"No. It doesn't. But at least you know it wasn't your fault."

Pradeep looked at him, really looked at him. "Why do you even care? You're management. You could just ignore this stuff like everyone else does."

Good question.

"Because," Ramesh said slowly, "someone should. And apparently, I'm the idiot who volunteered."

That evening, Ramesh sat in his car in the parking lot for twenty minutes before starting the engine.

His phone had six missed calls from his wife. Two texts from his credit card company. One email from corporate about mandatory expense reduction training.

He was exhausted in a way that went deeper than just physical tiredness. It was the exhaustion of holding things together that wanted to fall apart. Of making people laugh when he wanted to scream. Of pretending everything was manageable when it very clearly wasn't.

His phone rang. His wife.

"Hey," he answered.

"Where are you?"

"Sitting in the parking lot at work."

"Are you coming home?"

Was he? Home meant facing bills he couldn't pay, a daughter who wanted things he couldn't afford, a wife who was tired of his jokes and his avoidance and his inability to just be serious for once in his life.

"Yeah," he said. "I'm coming."

"Ramesh? Are you okay?"

"Of course. Why wouldn't I be?"

A long pause on the other end.

"You know you don't have to always be funny, right? You're allowed to just be sad sometimes."

The words hit him harder than they should have.

"I know," he said quietly.

But he didn't know. Not really. Because he'd spent so long being the person who made things lighter that he'd forgotten how to be anything else. The jokes weren't just for other people anymore—they were armor, protection, the wall between him and the reality that they were all going down and his humor couldn't stop it.

"Come home," his wife said. "We'll figure it out."

"Figure what out?"

"Everything. All of it. Together."

Ramesh closed his eyes. "Okay."

He hung up. Started the car. The grinding noise was definitely worse.

As he pulled out of the parking lot, he passed Arvind walking to his car, that leather notebook tucked under his arm. They made eye contact. Arvind nodded. Ramesh waved.

Two completely different people, dealing with the same disaster in completely different ways. One by observing, one by deflecting. Both equally useless in their own ways.

The guard at the gate saluted as Ramesh drove through.

"Goodnight, sir!"

"Goodnight! Try not to let the place burn down before tomorrow!"

The guard laughed.

Ramesh's smile dropped the second he was out of sight.

He drove home through traffic that never seemed to end, his mind full of things he couldn't fix and people he couldn't help and jokes that didn't land anymore, wondering when exactly he'd turned into this—a man who made everyone else feel better while slowly drowning himself.

But tomorrow he'd show up again. Crack jokes again. Make people laugh again.

Because someone had to.

And he was too far into the role to quit now.

Even if the role was killing him.

PART II

THE COST BEGINS

5

PRESSURE POINTS

Meera Kapoor learned to make decisions fast when her father had his heart attack.

She was twenty-three, fresh out of engineering college, standing in a hospital corridor while a doctor asked her questions that should have been for her mother—except her mother was having a panic attack in the waiting room and her older brother was stuck in Dubai and couldn't get a flight until tomorrow.

"We need to operate now," the doctor said. "There's risk, obviously, but waiting is riskier. You're the eldest present. We need consent."

"How much risk?"

"Twenty percent mortality rate. Eighty percent if we don't operate."

It wasn't really a choice. But it felt like one—signing papers that said you agreed your father might die on the table, that you made the call, that if it went wrong, it would be your decision that killed him.

He survived. Barely. But Meera learned something in that hospital corridor that most people never learn: when you're the one who has to choose, you stop having the luxury of doubt. You look at the options, pick the least terrible one, and live with the consequences.

Seventeen years later, she was Operations Director at Apex Chemicals, standing at the whiteboard in her office at 6 47 AM, looking at a decision that made that hospital corridor feel simple by comparison.

On the left side of the board, she'd written:

OPTION A: SHUT DOWN REACTOR 3 FOR REPAIRS

• Timeline: 14 days minimum

• Cost: ₹18 lakhs (parts + labor + contractor fees)

• Impact: 30% production capacity loss during shutdown

• Risk: Miss Q1 targets, trigger penalty clauses with remaining clients

• Potential outcome: Corporate loses confidence, accelerates shutdown timeline

On the right side:

OPTION B: KEEP REACTOR 3 RUNNING

• Timeline: Push through Q1, reassess after

• Cost: ₹0 immediate (defer maintenance)

• Impact: Maintain production capacity

• Risk: Catastrophic failure = 100% downtime + safety incident + regulatory nightmare

• Potential outcome: Could be nothing. Could be everything.

Between them, in the middle, she'd drawn a large question mark.

Her coffee had gone cold an hour ago. She drank it anyway.

The engineering report sat on her desk, flagged with red tabs on the relevant pages. She'd read it four times. The conclusion was clear: Reactor 3's cooling system was operating at 67% efficiency and degrading. The metallurgy on the main chamber showed stress fractures. The pressure regulation valve was "functioning but unreliable."

In engineering speak, that meant: this thing is going to fail. The only question is when.

But "when" was everything.

If it failed after Q1, after they'd hit their production numbers and potentially won back some client confidence, they might survive the repair timeline. Corporate might give them breathing room. The financial bleeding might slow enough to stop.

If she shut it down now, they'd miss targets by miles. Corporate would see "failing to meet commitments." The clients they were desperately trying to keep would start making contingency plans. The death spiral would accelerate.

A decision with perfect information would be easy. But she didn't have perfect information. She had engineering estimates ("could fail in 2-8 weeks") and financial projections ("we're dead if we miss targets") and corporate pressure ("deliver or we're done") and safety regulations ("if someone gets hurt, you go to jail").

All of it contradictory. All of it her responsibility.

Her phone buzzed. A message from Arvind:

Need to discuss Reactor 3 situation. Have you seen the latest sensor data?

Of course he'd seen it. Arvind saw everything. And he'd want to talk about failure probability distributions and risk matrices and gathering more data before deciding, because that's what Arvind did—he analyzed until the decision made itself or became irrelevant.

She didn't respond yet.

The morning production meeting was at 8:30. She had an hour and forty-three minutes to decide which disaster she was choosing.

At 7:15, she walked the reactor floor.

This was her habit—before big decisions, she came down here. Not to talk to anyone, just to see. To remember that the spreadsheets in her office represented real machines operated by real people whose real lives depended on what she chose.

Reactor 3 was running. From the outside, it looked fine—no smoke, no alarms, just the steady hum of chemicals cooking at precisely controlled temperatures. You'd never know it was dying.

But Meera knew. She'd been doing this long enough to hear the subtle changes in the sound, see the way operators kept adjusting parameters that should have been stable, notice the increased monitoring frequency that meant people were nervous.

Prakash was on duty, making his rounds. He saw her and straightened up slightly—that instinctive response everyone had when senior management showed up unannounced.

"Morning, ma'am."

"Morning, Prakash. How's she running?"

"Reactor 3? Fine, ma'am. All parameters within range."

"Within range" was doing a lot of work in that sentence. Meera pulled out her phone, opened the real-time monitoring app, and looked at the temperature curves. Technically within acceptable limits, yes. But jagged, inconsistent, requiring constant manual adjustment.

"You having to babysit her more than usual?"

Prakash hesitated, then nodded. "A little. The cooling system's... temperamental. But we're managing."

"How much longer can you manage?"

He understood what she was really asking. "Honestly? I don't know, ma'am. Could be fine for months. Could be tomorrow. The equipment's old, and we're pushing it hard."

"If you had to guess?"

"I don't like to guess with equipment that could fail explosive."

Smart answer. Diplomatic. Completely unhelpful for decision-making purposes.

"If someone forced you to guess."

Prakash looked at Reactor 3, then back at her. "Two weeks. Maybe three. That's just my feeling, not science."

Two to three weeks would get them to the end of Q1. Barely.

"Thank you for being honest."

"Are we shutting her down, ma'am?"

"I don't know yet."

"Can I say something?" Prakash asked, then continued without waiting for permission. "Whatever you decide, just... decide. This in-between thing where we're all waiting and watching—it's harder than either option. Just make the call and tell us so we can plan."

Meera studied him. Late forties, been here since the plant opened, probably knew these reactors better than anyone including the engineers who designed them. And he was right—the uncertainty was torture. For everyone.

"I'll decide today," she promised.

Back in her office, Meera found three people waiting: Arvind, Vikram, and Rajesh.

Great. The trifecta of opposing viewpoints.

"We need to talk about Reactor 3," Arvind said immediately.

"I'm aware."

"Have you made a decision?"

"Not yet."

Vikram jumped in. "Then let me make it simple for you: shut it down, we're dead. Keep it running, we have a chance. Easy choice."

"It's not an easy choice," Arvind said. "The failure risk is—"

"—acceptable," Vikram interrupted. "Everything has risk. The question is which risk kills us slower."

"Spoken like someone who's never had to explain a workplace fatality to someone's family."

"Spoken like someone who's never had to explain eight hundred layoffs to families who won't have income."

Rajesh, who'd been leaning against the wall, spoke up. "If I may offer a third option—we keep Reactor 3 running AND start negotiations with the backup supplier I mentioned. Position ourselves to absorb a shutdown if it happens, but don't voluntarily choose it. Best of both worlds."

Arvind turned to him. "Your backup supplier can't possibly ramp up fast enough to cover a thirty percent capacity loss."

"Not immediately, no. But in two to three weeks? Possibly. Especially if we pay premium rates."

"Which we can't afford."

"We can't afford a shutdown either, so pick your financial poison."

Meera held up her hand. "Everyone stop."

They stopped.

She walked to her whiteboard, the one with her two options still written on it. "Here's what I know: Arvind's right that the engineering risk is real. Vikram's right that the financial risk of shutdown is catastrophic. Rajesh's right that we need contingency planning. You're all right, and you're all wrong, and none of you are the ones who have to sign the decision memo that corporate will crucify me with if this goes bad."

Silence.

"So here's what we're going to do," Meera continued. "I'm going to make a decision by end of today. Not because I have perfect information—I'll never have that. But because this state of prolonged uncertainty is destroying morale and operational efficiency. Whatever I decide, we commit to it fully. No second-guessing, no 'I told you so,' no undermining. We execute as a team or we don't execute at all. Clear?"

Nods around the room, some more reluctant than others.

"Now get out. All of you. I need to think."

After they left, Meera sat at her desk and pulled out her phone. She scrolled to a contact she hadn't called in six months: her father.

He answered on the third ring. "Meera?"

"Hi, Papa."

"This is a surprise. You usually only call on Sundays."

"I know. Sorry. I've been..."

"Busy. I know. How's work?"

How was work? Collapsing. Burning. Impossible.

"Challenging," she said.

"Ah. That tone. What's the decision?"

Her father knew her too well. He'd been in manufacturing management for thirty years before retiring—different industry, same problems. Same impossible choices between bad and worse.

"Shut down critical equipment for repairs and miss targets, or keep running and risk catastrophic failure."

A long pause on the other end. Then: "What does your gut say?"

"My gut says I'm going to be wrong either way."

Her father laughed, but not unkindly. "That's usually the sign you're in real leadership territory. The easy decisions don't require you. It's the impossible ones that separate managers from leaders."

"Not helpful, Papa."

"I'm not trying to be helpful. You don't need help—you need permission to trust yourself. So here it is: you've analyzed the data, you've consulted the experts, you've considered the consequences. Now make the call and live with it. That's the job."

"And if I'm wrong?"

"Then you're wrong. But at least you made a decision based on the best information available at the time. That's all anyone can ask."

After she hung up, Meera sat there for a long time.

Then she picked up her pen and wrote on the whiteboard, in the space beneath the question mark:

DECISION: Shut down Reactor 3. Effective immediately.

Her hand shook slightly as she wrote it.

She pulled up her computer, opened the decision memo template, and started typing:

Effective 13:00 today, Reactor 3 will be taken offline for comprehensive maintenance and repair. Estimated timeline: 14-16 days. This decision is based on engineering assessment indicating high probability of catastrophic failure if operation continues. While this will impact Q1 production targets by approximately 30%, the alternative risk of unplanned failure, potential safety incident, and complete operational shutdown is unacceptable.

This is a proactive decision made with full consideration of financial impact. It is the right call.

That last line—*it is the right call*—was for her as much as for anyone who'd read it.

She sent the memo to the full leadership team and corporate. Immediate responses started flooding in.

From Vikram: **You just killed us. Hope you're happy.**

From Kavita: **This was brave. The workers will appreciate that you prioritized their safety.**

From Arvind: **Agree with this decision. I'll send you the detailed monitoring protocol we should implement during the shutdown.**

From Rajesh: **I'll accelerate supplier negotiations. We'll need backup capacity ASAP.**

From corporate: **Noted. We expect detailed daily updates on repair timeline and plan to recover lost production. No excuses.**

Meera forwarded the memo to floor supervisors and put out a plant-wide announcement:

All personnel: Reactor 3 will undergo scheduled maintenance shutdown beginning 1 PM today. This is a planned outage. Safety is our top priority. Production schedules will be adjusted accordingly. Thank you for your continued dedication.

She didn't mention that this "scheduled" maintenance had been decided thirty minutes ago, or that it was going to tank their quarterly numbers, or that corporate was going to use this as ammunition against them.

Just: *Safety is our top priority.*

True enough.

At 12:45 PM, Meera went down to the reactor floor to watch the shutdown herself.

The operators had been notified. Procedure required a two-hour shutdown sequence, but Meera had authorized an expedited four-hour version given the equipment's condition. Prakash was leading the team, walking through the step-by-step process of safely winding down a chemical reactor that had been running nonstop for three months.

Meera stood on the observation deck, watching the temperature gauges slowly decline, the pressure equalize, the feeds shut off one by one. It was strangely peaceful—this enormous piece of industrial equipment gently going to sleep.

Kavita appeared beside her.

"You made the right call," Kavita said quietly.

"We'll see."

"No, I mean it. Whatever happens with the numbers, you chose people over metrics. That matters."

"Does it? If we lose the plant, everyone loses their jobs anyway. I'm not sure I chose people—I just chose a different way of failing them."

Kavita didn't have a response to that.

They stood there together, watching Reactor 3 power down, the floor around it gradually emptying as operators moved to other stations, the giant yellow chamber finally going still and silent.

At 4:47 PM, engineering began the detailed teardown inspection.

At 6:23 PM, the lead engineer called Meera.

"Ma'am, you need to see this."

She went down immediately.

The reactor chamber was open, the inner walls exposed. The engineering team stood around it with flashlights and inspection tools, their expressions grim.

"Show me," Meera said.

The lead engineer pointed to a series of fractures in the metal lining—thin cracks spider-webbing across a section about two feet wide.

"This would have failed," he said quietly. "Not 'might have.' Would have. These stress fractures were millimeters from full breach. If we'd kept running—especially under load—this chamber would have ruptured within seventy-two hours. Maybe sooner."

"What would that have looked like?"

"Best case? Complete loss of batch, toxic fumes, emergency evacuation, HAZMAT response, regulatory investigation, probably six months shutdown for inspection and penalties. Worst case? Explosion, casualties, criminal charges."

The room went very quiet.

"Seventy-two hours," Meera repeated.

"Give or take. You shut it down just in time."

Meera stared at the fractured metal, at the disaster that had been hours away from happening, at the decision that had felt impossible this morning and now felt like the most obvious thing in the world.

She'd been right.

By accident or instinct or luck—she'd been right.

But she'd also been wrong. Because if she'd made this call two weeks ago when the first warning signs appeared, they could have done planned maintenance without the emergency rush. If she'd been more decisive earlier, less worried about the financial implications, less paralyzed by competing pressures...

Being right didn't mean she'd done it right.

"Document everything," she told the engineering team. "Photos, measurements, materials analysis. I want a complete report for corporate and regulatory."

"Yes, ma'am."

She walked back to her office through the darkening plant, past workers on second shift who didn't yet know how close they'd come to catastrophe, past reactors still running because they were safer than Reactor 3 had been, past the observation deck where she'd stood this morning weighing impossible choices.

Her phone buzzed. A message from Vikram:

Heard about the fractures. You got lucky.

She typed back: **Lucky is still alive. I'll take it.**

Another message, this one from corporate:

Your decision memo regarding Reactor 3 has been reviewed. Given the subsequent engineering findings, we're updating our maintenance protocols across all facilities. Good catch.

Not an apology for the pressure they'd put on her. Not an acknowledgment that they'd have crucified her if she'd shut it down without the dramatic fracture evidence.

Just*Good catch.*

As if she'd spotted a typo in an email instead of prevented a potential disaster.

Meera forwarded the engineering photos to the full leadership team with a single line:

This is what we were 72 hours away from. Decisions have consequences. So does indecision.

Then she shut down her computer, turned off her office lights, and went home.

Her husband was already asleep. Her daughter's bedroom light was still on—probably reading past her bedtime again.

Meera stood in the kitchen, finally allowing herself to feel the full weight of the day. The terror of the choice. The relief of being right. The exhaustion of carrying the responsibility alone.

Tomorrow, corporate would push for faster repairs. Vikram would complain about lost production. Clients would threaten to take their business elsewhere. The financial pressure would continue, relentless and suffocating.

But tonight, Reactor 3 sat safely silent, being repaired instead of exploding.

Tonight, no one was hurt.

Tonight, her decision had been right.

And for once, that was enough.

6

RUST IN THE SYSTEM

Vikram Rao believed in natural selection.

Not the Darwin kind—though he'd read *Origin of Species* twice and thought the old man was onto something. No, Vikram believed in corporate natural selection: the strong survived, the weak got fired, and anyone who couldn't handle pressure had no business being in manufacturing in the first place.

He'd learned this at twenty-six, working his first supervisory role at a textile mill in Surat. His manager then—a soft-spoken man named Krishnan who everyone loved—spent six months trying to coach an underperforming worker, giving him chance after chance, extra training, modified duties, encouragement.

The worker never improved. But he also never got fired, because Krishnan "believed in people" and "saw potential."

Meanwhile, the rest of the team had to carry his weight. Overtime increased. Mistakes multiplied. Good workers started leaving because they were tired of compensating for someone who shouldn't have been there in the first place.

Eventually, corporate fired Krishnan for missing targets. The underperforming worker quit three weeks later anyway.

The lesson was clear: being nice didn't save anyone. It just delayed the inevitable and took everyone else down in the process.

Vikram had never forgotten that.

Now, at forty-seven, he was the Plant Operations Manager at Apex Chemicals, and he ran his department the way you ran anything that needed to survive: ruthlessly, efficiently, without sentiment or apology.

People called him a ruthless. He called it accountability.

He arrived at 6:00 AM sharp, like always. Not because he loved the job—though he was good at it—but because arriving early meant you saw who else arrived early (ambitious, useful) and who dragged in at the last minute (lazy, expendable).

This morning, he found three operators clustered near the entrance, talking in low voices. They went quiet when they saw him.

Red flag.

"Morning," Vikram said, not slowing down. "We're paying you to stand around gossiping, or were you planning to actually work today?"

The youngest one—Amit, maybe twenty-four—flinched. "We were just—"

"I don't care what you were 'just.' You're on the clock in seven minutes. Be at your stations or don't bother showing up."

He walked past without waiting for a response.

In his office, Vikram pulled up the previous day's production reports. Reactor Hall B: efficiency down to 71%. Three batches flagged for quality review. Two equipment malfunctions, both classified as "operator error."

Operator error. The polite way of saying someone screwed up.

He made a note: *Review Reactor Hall B staffing. Identify bottom 15%. Prepare documentation for termination.*

His phone buzzed. A message from Dinesh, the floor supervisor:

Pradeep called out again. Third time this month. We're short-staffed on Line 4.

Vikram typed back: **Write him up. Three strikes protocol. Start looking for replacement.**

He said his kid is sick.

Not our problem.

He could practically feel Dinesh's hesitation through the screen, but eventually a response came back:

Understood.

This was the problem with modern management—everyone wanted to treat a chemical plant like a therapy center. Someone's kid was sick? That's unfortunate. Someone's car broke down? That's tough. Someone's having "personal issues"? Join the club.

But none of those things changed the fact that chemicals needed to be produced, standards needed to be met, and clients needed their orders on time. Either you showed up and did your job, or you got out of the way for someone who would.

The morning production briefing was at 8:00. Vikram walked in to find the usual suspects: Meera looking exhausted, Arvind with his leather notebook, Kavita radiating her typical bleeding-heart concern for everyone, Rajesh checking his phone, Ramesh probably preparing whatever stupid joke he'd use to deflect from real issues.

Meera started with the Reactor 3 update. Shutdown going as planned, engineering had found the stress fractures, everyone should feel good about dodging a disaster.

Vikram listened with his arms crossed.

When she finished, he spoke up. "So now we're thirty percent down on capacity because we have equipment that should have been replaced five years ago but wasn't because someone decided maintenance wasn't a priority."

"We made the right call," Meera said firmly. "The reactor was going to fail."

"I'm not questioning the shutdown. I'm questioning how we got to the point where emergency shutdown was our only option. This is what happens when we don't maintain standards, when we let things slide, when we're more worried about hurting people's feelings than running a functional operation."

"That's not fair," Kavita said. "The equipment degradation has nothing to do with—"

"It has everything to do with it. We've been babying failing systems—equipment and people—for months instead of making hard calls. And now we're paying for it."

Arvind spoke up, calm as always. "The maintenance schedule was approved by corporate. This isn't a floor management issue."

"No, but the operational efficiency is. And efficiency is trash because we have operators who can't be bothered to show up consistently, supervisors who won't enforce basic standards, and management"—he looked around the table—"that's too scared to actually manage."

"Meaning?" Meera's voice had an edge now.

"Meaning we need to cut the dead weight. Twenty percent workforce reduction, starting with the worst performers. Clean house. Bring in people who actually want to be here."

"We just lost Reactor 3," Priya said, her voice careful. "You want to add a mass layoff on top of that? You'll destroy what's left of morale."

"Morale doesn't produce chemicals. Competent workers do."

"Competent workers who are terrified and demoralized don't produce chemicals either."

Vikram leaned forward. "You know what terrifies workers? Unemployment. Which is what they'll all face if this plant closes because we were too soft to make necessary cuts."

The argument spiraled from there—the same circular debate they'd been having for weeks. Kavita defending the workers, Priya talking about team cohesion, Rajesh trying to redirect to financial strategies, Dev suggesting technological solutions nobody wanted to fund.

Vikram stopped listening halfway through. He'd made his point. Whether they agreed or not was irrelevant—he'd do what needed to be done in his department regardless.

After the meeting, he went straight to Dinesh.

"Conference room. Now."

Dinesh followed, looking nervous. Good. People should be nervous around him. Kept them sharp.

Vikram closed the door and pulled out his tablet, opening a spreadsheet. "Performance metrics for Reactor Hall B. Last thirty days."

Dinesh glanced at the numbers and winced.

"Talk to me about these efficiency ratings," Vikram said. "Seventy-one percent average. Target is eighty-five. That's not a small miss."

"We've had equipment issues, staffing shortages because of call-outs, the Reactor 3 situation affecting workflow—"

"Excuses. I'm asking for explanation, not excuses."

Dinesh's jaw tightened. "With respect, sir, those aren't excuses. They're the actual operational challenges we're dealing with."

"And whose job is it to manage those challenges?"

"Mine."

"Exactly. So when I see numbers like this, what I'm really seeing is supervision failure. Your failure."

Silence. Dinesh stared at the tablet screen, face flushed.

"Here's what's going to happen," Vikram continued. "You have two weeks to get Reactor Hall B back above eighty percent efficiency. I don't care how you do it—extended shifts, reassignments, performance improvement plans, terminations. But the numbers move up, or you move out. Clear?"

"Sir, two weeks isn't"

"Two weeks. Not negotiable."

Dinesh nodded stiffly and left without another word.

Vikram sat back in his chair. Was he being harsh? Yes. Was it necessary? Absolutely.

You didn't fix a failing operation by being understanding. You fixed it by setting clear expectations, demanding results, and removing obstacles—including human ones.

At 11:30, Vikram did his floor walk.

This was his favorite part of the day—not because he enjoyed the noise and heat, but because you couldn't hide on the floor. In meetings, people could bullshit. In emails, they could deflect. But on the floor, incompetence was visible.

He watched an operator named Sunil fumbling with a valve adjustment on Reactor 7. Three attempts, each time overshooting the target pressure.

Vikram walked over. "Problem?"

Sunil jumped slightly. "No, sir. Just—the valve's sticking a bit. I'm adjusting."

"I can see that. What I'm asking is why you're adjusting manually when the automated system should be handling it."

"The automation's been glitchy lately, so I've been doing it by hand to be safe."

"And you reported the glitch to engineering?"

Sunil hesitated. "I... mentioned it to Dinesh."

"When?"

"Last week?"

"And?"

"He said he'd look into it."

Vikram made a mental note: *Dinesh not following up on equipment issues. Add to documentation.*

"From now on," Vikram said, "you report technical problems directly to engineering. Copy your supervisor. I want a paper trail for everything that's broken around here."

"Yes, sir."

Vikram continued his walk, cataloging issues: a leaking seal on Reactor 5 that should have been replaced yesterday, contaminated tools left out instead of being properly cleaned, safety equipment stored incorrectly.

Each one a small thing. Each one a sign of slipping standards.

He found Dinesh near the break room, talking to a group of operators. They were laughing about something—Dinesh doing his version of "connecting with the team," probably.

"Dinesh. A word."

Dinesh followed him to a quieter corner, the laughter dying behind them.

"Sunil told me he reported a faulty automation system last week. You were supposed to follow up with engineering. Did you?"

Dinesh's expression flickered—caught. "I... it's been busy, sir. It's on my list."

"Your list. Meanwhile, we have an operator manually adjusting critical parameters because automated systems aren't working. You see the problem?"

"I'll submit the work order today."

"You should have submitted it last week. This is exactly what I'm talking about—lack of follow-through, lack of accountability. You're managing by hoping problems solve themselves."

"With respect, sir, I'm managing thirty-seven people across three shifts with equipment that's falling apart and targets that keep increasing. I'm doing the best I can."

"Your best isn't good enough."

The words landed hard. Dinesh's face went through several expressions—anger, hurt, resignation.

"I've been doing this job for twelve years," Dinesh said quietly. "I've never had complaints until"

"Until standards started mattering. Yes. That's the point. We've been coasting on 'good enough' for too long. That stops now."

Vikram walked away, leaving Dinesh standing there.

Was it harsh? Yes. Did Dinesh deserve some recognition for his years of service? Maybe. But recognition didn't fix faulty automation systems or improve efficiency ratings.

Results did.

At 3:00 PM, Vikram's phone rang. HR.

"Mr. Rao, we need to discuss something. Can you come down?"

He went, already knowing what this was about. There were only so many aggressive management conversations you could have before someone complained.

The HR manager—Shweta, mid-thirties, perpetually uncomfortable with conflict—gestured to a chair. "Please, sit."

"I'd rather stand. What's this about?"

"We've received three complaints in the past week regarding your management style. I'm required to discuss them with you."

"Complaints from whom?"

"That's confidential. But the issues raised include inappropriate tone, public criticism of staff, creating a hostile work environment"

"Let me guess," Vikram interrupted. "These complaints came after I started actually holding people accountable for their performance?"

Shweta shifted uncomfortably. "The timing may be coincidental."

"It's not coincidental. It's predictable. The moment you expect standards, people cry 'hostile environment.' The moment you give critical feedback, it's 'inappropriate tone.' This is what happens when you've let people underperform for years—they think accountability is abuse."

"Mr. Rao, regardless of the motivation behind the complaints, I'm obligated to address them. Your management approach is creating friction—"

"My management approach is the only thing keeping this department functional. You want me to be nicer? Fine. I'll be nice. And in three months when we've lost every remaining client because production has completely collapsed, we can all hold hands and feel good about how respectful we were while the company died."

"That's not what I'm saying."

"Then what are you saying?"

Shweta took a breath. "I'm saying there's a difference between high standards and aggressive behavior. You can demand excellence without making people feel worthless."

"Can you? Because in my experience, people who feel 'worthless' when you point out their failures are usually people who should feel that way. Not because they're inherently bad, but because they're failing and need to either fix it or leave."

"That's... that's quite a perspective."

"It's reality. Look, I get it—I'm not winning any popularity contests. I'm fine with that. My job isn't to be liked. It's to keep this operation running. And right now, being liked and being effective are mutually exclusive."

Shweta made some notes in her file. "I'm going to document this conversation. I'd recommend you consider adjusting your communication style. But ultimately, it's your choice."

"Noted."

He left HR, his mood darkening. This was the problem—the moment you actually tried to fix things, people fought back. Not because your approach was wrong, but because change was uncomfortable and accountability was scary.

That evening, Vikram was reviewing termination documentation for three underperforming operators when his phone rang. His daughter.

"Hey, beta."

"Papa, are you coming to my recital tomorrow?"

Shit. He'd forgotten. Again.

"What time is it?"

"Six PM. At my school. You promised you'd come this time."

He pulled up his calendar. Tomorrow at 6:00 he had a production review meeting with corporate—the one he'd scheduled specifically to discuss the Reactor 3 situation and defend his department's performance metrics.

"Beta, I have an important meeting"

"You always have an important meeting."

"This one is really critical. The company is"

"I don't care about the company!" Her voice cracked. "I just want my dad to show up for once. Like other kids' dads do."

Silence on both ends.

"I'll try," Vikram said finally. "I can't promise, but I'll try."

"You won't come. You never do."

She hung up.

Vikram sat there, phone in hand, feeling something uncomfortable twist in his chest.

When had he last gone to one of her events? Her birthday was three months ago—he'd been there for dinner but left early for a supplier crisis. The school function before that? He'd missed it entirely because of a quality audit.

He told himself it was necessary. Someone had to keep the company running. Someone had to make the hard calls and put in the extra hours and sacrifice personal comfort for professional duty.

But sitting alone in his office at 7:30 PM, reviewing documents to fire people who probably had daughters who had recitals too,

Vikram wondered when exactly he'd become the kind of person his own daughter couldn't count on.

The kind of person nobody wanted to be around.

The kind of person who was right about everything and wrong about what mattered.

His phone buzzed. A message from Dinesh:

Submitted my resignation. Effective two weeks. Can't do this anymore. Good luck.

Vikram stared at the message.

Dinesh was the third supervisor to quit in four months. All of them citing "management style differences" in their exit interviews. All of them competent people who couldn't handle the pressure—or couldn't handle him.

He should feel vindicated. Weak links removing themselves, just like he'd told Kavita. Natural selection in action.

Instead, he felt something else. Something he didn't have a name for.

He opened his laptop and pulled up Dinesh's file. Twelve years of service. Generally solid performance until the last year when everything started falling apart. Recently flagged for follow-up issues, true, but before that? Consistent, reliable, respected by his team.

Had Vikram broken him? Or had Dinesh always been weak, just finally exposed by increased pressure?

Did it matter?

Vikram typed a response: **Understood. HR will process your paperwork. Thank you for your service.**

Professional. Neutral. Exactly the tone appropriate for a resignation.

He hit send, then sat there staring at the screen.

Outside his window, the reactor floor glowed with activity. Second shift running at 73% efficiency—still below target, but better than yesterday. Workers moving through their routines, operating equipment, following procedures.

Good people, mostly. Doing difficult work in impossible conditions.

And he was supposed to make it work. Supposed to push them harder, demand more, accept less, drive efficiency up through sheer force of will and unwillingness to accept failure.

That's what leadership meant, right? Making the hard calls. Being the bad guy so the company survived.

Right?

His phone buzzed again. This time, an email from corporate:

Followingrecent complaints regarding management practices in your department, we're implementing a mandatory leadership coaching program. Details to follow. This is not optional.

Leadership coaching. Translation: we think you're the problem.

Vikram closed his laptop.

He sat in his dark office for twenty more minutes, not working, not thinking, just sitting in the space between who he thought he was and who everyone else saw.

Then he stood up, turned off the lights, and drove home through traffic that never ended, past workers at bus stops heading home from their shifts, past shops closing for the night, past families eating dinner together through lit windows.

He got home at 9:15. His daughter's bedroom light was off. His wife was watching TV in the living room, barely looking up when he came in.

"There's food in the kitchen if you're hungry," she said.

"Thanks."

"Priya called earlier. Something about her recital."

"I know."

"Are you going?"

"I have a meeting."

His wife didn't respond. Just turned back to the TV.

Vikram stood there for a moment, briefcase in hand, tie loosened, exhausted in a way that went deeper than physical tiredness.

Then he went to his study, opened his laptop, and continued working on the termination documents.

Because someone had to.

Because results mattered.

Because being right was more important than being loved.

Right?

The cursor blinked on the screen, waiting for him to type the next name on the list of people who weren't good enough, weren't strong enough, weren't whatever enough to survive in the system he'd built.

Vikram stared at it, his hands on the keyboard, and for the first time in years, he hesitated.

Not because he was wrong.

But because being right was starting to feel an awful lot like being alone.

7

THE CHALLENGER RISES

Dev Malhotra was twenty-three when he realized the manufacturing world was run by people who were terrified of the future.

He'd just joined his first job—a mid-sized pharmaceutical plant in Hyderabad, fresh out of engineering college with a head full of automation theory and process optimization models. His first week, he'd identified seventeen inefficiencies in their production line. Simple fixes, most of them. Software updates, sensor recalibration, better data integration.

He wrote up a proposal. Six pages, complete with cost-benefit analysis and implementation timeline.

His supervisor—a man named Venkat who'd been doing the same job for twenty-two years—read it during their meeting, then set it down and said: "This is very thorough. Very impressive. Now let me tell you why we'll never do any of it."

"Why not?"

"Because if it works, great—you're the hero and I look like an idiot for not thinking of it first. And if it fails, I'm the idiot who approved it. Either way, I lose. So we'll keep doing what we've always done, because at least that way, when things go wrong, it's not my fault."

Dev had stared at him, genuinely confused. "But... don't you want things to get better?"

Venkat had smiled sadly. "Kid, in manufacturing, 'better' is the enemy of 'employed.' Remember that."

Nine years later, Dev was thirty-two and still hadn't learned to accept that logic.

He arrived at Apex Chemicals at 7:45 AM, laptop bag over his shoulder, wireless earbuds playing a podcast about machine learning applications in industrial automation. The future was happening everywhere except here, apparently.

The plant floor was already running—operators moving through routines that had been standardized in 1998 and hadn't changed since. Manual temperature checks that could be automated. Visual inspections that sensors could do better. Handwritten logs that should have been digitized a decade ago.

It was like watching people use typewriters in the age of computers. Functional, sure. But unnecessarily difficult and absurdly inefficient.

Dev's office was barely an office—more like a converted storage room with a desk and a window that overlooked the parking lot. He'd been promised "better accommodations" when he was hired eighteen months ago. Still waiting.

He opened his laptop and pulled up the automation proposal he'd been working on for three months. The one he'd presented twice already. The one that kept getting "tabled for further discussion."

APEX DIGITAL TRANSFORMATION INITIATIVEPhase 1: Reactor Lines 3 & 4

- Automated temperature and pressure monitoring
- Real-time quality analytics
- Predictive maintenance algorithms
- Estimated ROI: 18 months
- Estimated efficiency gain: 23-27%
- Initial investment: ₹47 lakhs

The numbers were solid. The technology was proven. Companies across India—across the world—were doing this already. But at Apex, suggesting anything new was treated like suggesting they all jump off a cliff together.

His phone buzzed. A message from Priya:

Leadership meeting at 9. Meera wants everyone there.

Dev typed back: **What's the agenda?**

The usual. Production numbers, crisis management, arguing about everything.

So a normal Tuesday.

Exactly.

Dev closed his laptop and headed to the conference room early. He wanted to set up his presentation before everyone arrived—assuming they'd even let him present this time.

The conference room was empty except for Arvind, who was already seated, leather notebook open, writing something in his precise handwriting.

"Morning, Arvind."

Arvind looked up, nodded. "Dev."

"You ever feel like we're rearranging deck chairs on the Titanic?"

"Every day," Arvind said calmly. "But I prefer to think of it as documenting the decline so historians can study what went wrong."

Dev laughed despite himself. "That's dark."

"That's realistic."

Dev plugged his laptop into the projector, pulling up his presentation. Charts showing current efficiency rates versus projected rates with automation. Photos of competing facilities that had already modernized. Testimonials from other companies that had made the leap.

Arvind watched quietly. "You're presenting the automation proposal again?"

"Third time's the charm?"

"Or the third time you get shot down."

"Optimism, Arvind. You should try it."

"I did. In 2019. It didn't work out."

The room started filling up. Meera arrived looking exhausted—which was her default these days. Kavita came in with that concerned expression she always wore, like she was carrying everyone's emotional weight. Vikram walked in radiating his usual aggressive energy. Rajesh slid in looking polished and unreadable. Ramesh wandered in mid-conversation with someone on his phone, laughing about something.

Suresh came in last, looking like he hadn't slept in days. Dev made a mental note to check in with him later—the procurement manager was clearly drowning.

Meera started the meeting with the Reactor 3 update. Still offline, repairs ahead of schedule, should be back online in ten days instead of fourteen. Good news, relatively speaking.

Then she moved to production targets. Bad news. They were going to miss Q1 projections by at least 22%, possibly more.

"Corporate is pushing for recovery plans," Meera said. "We need ideas. Real ones. Today."

This was Dev's opening.

"I have something," he said, pulling up his presentation. "If you'll give me ten minutes."

Meera gestured. "Go ahead."

Dev clicked to his first slide. **AUTOMATION: FROM COST TO INVESTMENT**

"We've been talking about automation for months, but we keep treating it like a luxury expense. It's not. It's a survival strategy. Every month we delay, we fall further behind competitors who are already doing this."

He clicked through slides showing efficiency comparisons, cost projections, implementation timelines.

"Reactor Lines 3 and 4 are the lowest-performing units. Perfect candidates for a pilot program. We install automated monitoring systems, integrate real-time analytics, implement predictive maintenance protocols. Initial investment is forty-seven lakhs, but the ROI is eighteen months. After that, we're looking at sustained twenty-five percent efficiency gains."

Vikram cut in. "Forty-seven lakhs we don't have, for technology that might work, requiring staff training we don't have time for, creating new failure points we can't afford. Hard pass."

"It's not 'might work'—it is working. At facilities just like ours. I can give you case studies from—"

"I don't care about case studies. I care about our reality. Which is that we're barely keeping the lights on, and you want to drop fifty lakhs on fancy computers."

"It's not fancy computers. It's modern manufacturing. This is standard practice everywhere except here."

Kavita spoke up, her voice careful. "Dev, I hear what you're saying. But Vikram's right that the timing is challenging. The workers are already stressed about job security. If we start automating, they'll think we're replacing them."

"We're not replacing them. We're enhancing their capabilities. Automation doesn't eliminate jobs—it eliminates the tedious, error-prone tasks so people can focus on higher-value work."

"That's a nice theory," Vikram said. "In practice, automation means fewer workers needed. Which, honestly, isn't the worst outcome given our current productivity issues."

"That's not—" Dev stopped, recalibrated. Getting angry wouldn't help. "Look, I'm not proposing this to eliminate jobs. I'm proposing it to save the plant. If we don't modernize, we'll lose to competitors who have. It's that simple."

Rajesh, who'd been quiet, finally spoke. "The fundamental problem isn't technology. It's capital. We don't have forty-seven lakhs lying around. Even if we did, corporate would never approve it right now—not with our current performance metrics."

"So we're trapped," Dev said. "Can't improve performance without investment, can't get investment without improving performance. Perfect circle of failure."

"Welcome to manufacturing," Ramesh said with a sad smile.

Arvind spoke up, measured as always. "Dev's analysis is sound. The ROI calculations are conservative. The technology is proven. But the implementation risk in our current state is significant. We're already dealing with Reactor 3 offline, staff morale issues, production pressure from corporate. Adding a major system change on top of that..."

"Is exactly what we need," Dev finished. "Because doing the same thing and expecting different results is insane."

"Or," Arvind said, "it's prudent risk management during crisis.

There's a difference between resistance to change and recognition of poor timing."

Dev felt his frustration building. This was the same wall he hit every time. Good arguments, reasonable concerns, and absolutely zero willingness to actually try anything different.

"So what's the alternative?" he asked. "Keep running 1990s technology and hope it magically becomes competitive? Keep manually checking systems that could monitor themselves? Keep losing clients because we're slower and less reliable than facilities that modernized years ago?"

Silence around the table.

Finally, Meera spoke. "Dev, I appreciate the proposal. I really do. But right now, with Reactor 3 down and corporate breathing down our necks, I can't justify a forty-seven lakh investment in unproven—"

"It's not unproven!"

"—in new systems that will require training and integration during our busiest period. The answer is no. Not now. Maybe in six months if things stabilize."

"In six months, we might not be here."

"Then we definitely won't need automation."

Dev closed his laptop, jaw tight. "This is a mistake."

"Noted," Meera said, not unkindly. "Next item—"

"No, I'm serious. You're all sitting here managing decline instead of actually trying to fix anything. Vikram wants to fire people. Kavita wants to comfort people. Arvind wants to study people. Rajesh wants to make deals with people. And nobody—nobody

—is willing to actually change the fundamental systems that are failing."

Vikram leaned forward. "Careful, kid. You're about five seconds from a very short career."

"What career? We're a sinking ship run by people who are more interested in protecting their positions than saving the company. I'm trying to offer solutions and getting shut down by—"

"Dev." Priya's voice cut through, firm but not harsh. "Take a breath."

He did. Forced himself to sit back, to unclench his fists, to remember that burning bridges wouldn't help his cause.

But the frustration remained, burning in his chest.

The meeting continued without him. He sat there, half-listening to the same circular arguments about cost-cutting and efficiency and maintaining morale. All symptoms, no diagnosis. All reaction, no strategy.

After the meeting ended, Priya caught up with him in the hallway.

"That was quite a show," she said.

"They're impossible."

"They're scared. There's a difference."

"Scared of what? Progress?"

"Scared of making things worse. Scared of spending money they don't have. Scared of change during a crisis when they can't afford failure. You're young, Dev. You don't remember what it's like when major changes go wrong."

"And you don't remember what it's like when refusing to change goes wrong. Because that's where we are."

Priya studied him for a moment. "You're not wrong about the automation. Your analysis is good, your technology is sound. But your timing is terrible, and your approach is worse."

"What's wrong with my approach?"

"You come in like a missionary trying to convert heathens. 'Here's the future, you're all backwards idiots for not seeing it.' That's not how you build support. That's how you create resistance."

"So I should what? Pretend we're doing fine? Sugarcoat the fact that we're using obsolete systems?"

"No. You should recognize that people have legitimate concerns, address them instead of dismissing them, and build coalitions instead of fighting everyone at once. Arvind might support you if you addressed his risk concerns. Kavita might support you if you showed how automation helps workers instead of replacing them. Even Vikram might support you if you framed it as competitive advantage instead of expensive experiment."

Dev wanted to argue, but he couldn't. She was right.

"I'm just tired of watching us fail slowly," he said quietly.

"I know. We all are. But the difference between a challenger and a rebel is that challengers build alternatives while rebels just burn things down. Which one are you?"

She walked away before he could answer.

Dev spent the rest of the morning at his desk, staring at his proposal, trying to figure out how to rebuild it with Priya's advice in mind.

The problem was, he was right. He knew he was right. The data supported it, the technology existed, the case studies were there. Automation wasn't some futuristic fantasy—it was current best practice that Apex was simply refusing to adopt.

But being right didn't matter if you couldn't convince anyone to act on it.

His phone buzzed. A message from an unknown number:

Your automation proposal is good. They won't approve it, but it's good. Keep pushing. Some of us are watching.

Dev stared at the message. Who was this? How did they get his number?

He typed back: **Who is this?**

No response.

Around 2:00 PM, Dev went down to the reactor floor. Not because he had specific work to do there, but because sitting in his converted-closet office was making him crazy.

He found himself near Reactor 4, watching operators manually log data that should have been automatically recorded. Every fifteen minutes, someone walked over, read gauges, wrote numbers in a logbook with a pen. Then someone else would come by later, transfer those numbers to a computer spreadsheet.

Two unnecessary steps. Two opportunities for human error. Two wastes of time and labor.

He approached one of the operators—Sunita, late thirties, been here for years.

"Can I ask you something?" Dev said.

Sunita looked up, surprised. "Sure, sir."

"How much of your shift is spent just recording data?"

She thought about it. "Maybe... thirty percent? Checking gauges, writing it down, double-checking numbers."

"And how often do you catch errors in the automated readings?"

"Not often. The sensors are usually pretty accurate. We're just required to verify manually."

"What if the system could do all of that automatically? Would that make your job easier or harder?"

Sunita's expression shifted to something cautious. "Are you asking if I want to be replaced by a computer?"

"No. I'm asking if you'd rather spend your time on actual problem-solving instead of data entry."

"I guess... easier? But also, if computers are doing everything, why do they need us?"

This was the fear Kavita had mentioned. The reasonable, human fear that automation meant elimination.

"Because computers can't think," Dev said. "They can monitor, record, flag anomalies. But they can't diagnose complex problems, can't make judgment calls, can't adapt to unexpected situations. That's what you do. Automation would just remove the boring parts so you can focus on the important parts."

"That sounds good in theory, sir. But in practice, when companies automate, people get laid off. We've all seen it."

"Not always. Sometimes people get retrained for higher-skilled positions."

"And sometimes they get told 'thank you for your service' and shown the door."

Dev didn't have a good response to that. Because she was right—sometimes that is what happened.

"I don't want anyone to lose their jobs," he said finally. "I want the plant to survive. And I think automation is part of how we do that."

Sunita nodded politely, but her expression said she didn't quite believe him.

As Dev walked away, he realized the problem was bigger than just convincing management. He had to convince the workers that change was protection, not threat. That modernization was survival, not elimination.

That was a much harder sell.

That evening, Dev stayed late, working on a revised proposal that incorporated Priya's feedback. Less missionary, more diplomat. Address concerns, build coalitions, frame it properly.

He was deep into cost-benefit scenarios when his phone rang. His girlfriend, Ananya.

"Hey," he answered.

"You're still at work, aren't you?"

"How did you—"

"Because you're always still at work. Dev, it's 8:30. You were supposed to meet me for dinner at 7:00."

Shit. He'd completely forgotten.

"I'm sorry. I got caught up in—"

"In saving the world through automation. I know. You're always caught up in something."

There was an edge in her voice that Dev recognized. This wasn't just about missed dinner.

"Ananya—"

"Do you ever stop and wonder if maybe you're fighting a battle that can't be won? That maybe this place doesn't want to be saved?"

"Someone has to try."

"Why does it have to be you?"

Good question. Why did it have to be him?

"Because I can see the solution. I can see exactly what needs to change, and I can't just... ignore that. I can't watch something fail when I know how to fix it."

"Even if fixing it means sacrificing everything else? Your relationships, your health, your happiness?"

"I'm not sacrificing—"

"You are. You're so focused on this crusade that you're forgetting there's a life outside of it. We haven't had a real conversation in weeks. You missed my sister's wedding last month because of some work crisis. You're constantly stressed, constantly angry at people who won't listen to you, constantly—"

"I'm trying to make a difference!"

"But at what cost?"

Silence on both ends.

"I need to think about some things," Ananya said finally. "And you need to think about what you're really fighting for—the company, or your own need to be right."

She hung up.

Dev sat there, phone in hand, the words hitting harder than he wanted to admit.

Your own need to be right.

Was that what this was? He told himself it was about saving the plant, helping the workers, modernizing a failing system. But was it really? Or was it about proving that he was smarter than the old guard, that his way was better, that he was right and they were wrong?

He looked at his revised proposal on the screen. Sixty-three slides, every objection addressed, every concern acknowledged, every number verified.

It was perfect.

And it probably wouldn't matter.

Dev closed his laptop and sat in his dark office, looking out at the parking lot where only a few cars remained. Night shift starting, day shift ended hours ago, and here he was—thirty-two years old, fighting battles nobody asked him to fight, losing relationships over principles that might not even be principles.

Just stubbornness wrapped in righteousness.

He thought about Sunita's question: *Why do they need us?*

And Ananya's question: *Why does it have to be you?*

And Priya's question: *Which one are you—challenger or rebel?*

Dev didn't have good answers to any of them.

But tomorrow, he'd try again. Present the proposal again. Make the case again. Push for change again.

Because what else was he supposed to do? Accept defeat? Watch the plant fail without trying? Become like Arvind, observing from a distance? Like Ramesh, making jokes while everything burned? Like Vikram, breaking people in the name of results?

No.

He'd keep challenging. Keep pushing. Keep fighting for the future even if nobody wanted it.

Even if it cost him everything.

Even if he was wrong about why he was doing it.

Dev packed up his laptop and headed to his car, driving home through streets he barely saw, his mind already working on tomorrow's argument, tomorrow's approach, tomorrow's battle in a war he might be fighting alone.

The future was coming whether Apex was ready or not.

Dev just had to figure out if he was trying to save them from it or prove that he was right about it.

There was probably a difference.

He just wasn't sure he knew what it was anymore.

PART III

COLLISION COURSE

8

THE COST OF CARING

Suresh Iyer discovered he was having a panic attack in aisle 7 of the More Megastore at 9:47 PM on a Tuesday.

He'd stopped on the way home to buy milk—just milk, one simple task—and found himself standing in front of the dairy section unable to remember why he was there. His heart was hammering. His hands were shaking. The fluorescent lights felt too bright, the store too loud, the choices too many.

Failure plants a permanent weight in the chest.

Full cream or toned? One liter or two? Glass bottle or plastic pouch?

His brain couldn't process it. Couldn't make the decision. Couldn't do this one simple thing that every person did every day without thinking about it.

He stood there for eleven minutes, frozen, while other shoppers moved around him, until a store employee asked if he needed help and Suresh heard himself say "I'm fine" in a voice that didn't sound like his own.

He left without buying anything.

That was three weeks ago.

Since then, things had gotten worse.

Now it was 4:47 AM and Suresh was already awake, lying in bed, staring at the ceiling, his mind cycling through the same thoughts it had been cycling through for hours:

Reactor 3 is down, which means suppliers need to adjust delivery schedules, which means renegotiating timelines, which means at least forty phone calls today, which means forty conversations where he has to sound competent and confident when he feels neither, which means...

His wife stirred beside him. "You're awake again."

"Sorry. Didn't mean to wake you."

"You didn't. Your breathing changes when you're anxious. It's been different for weeks now."

Suresh didn't respond. What was he supposed to say? *Yes, I'm drowning. Yes, I can't handle my job anymore. Yes, I'm failing at everything and everyone can see it.*

"You should talk to someone," she said quietly. "A doctor. A therapist. Someone."

"I'm fine."

"You're not fine. You're barely sleeping. You're barely eating. Yesterday you snapped at Aarav for asking about his school project."

Guilt twisted in Suresh's stomach. His son was nine. The project wasn't even complicated—something about the solar system. But when Aarav had asked for help, Suresh had felt such overwhelming irritation that he'd said "Ask your mother, I'm busy" in a tone sharp enough that Aarav's face had crumpled.

He'd apologized later. Aarav had said it was okay. But kids always said it was okay when it wasn't.

"I'll talk to someone," Suresh lied. "After things calm down at work."

"When will that be?"

Never, probably. But he said, "Soon."

He got up at 5:15, showered in water that never felt quite the right temperature, dressed in clothes that fit wrong even though they were the same size they'd always been, and drove to work through morning traffic that made him want to scream.

By 6:30 AM, he was at his desk, staring at his inbox: 147 unread emails.

He'd gone through 89 of them yesterday. Apparently, 147 new ones had arrived overnight.

Suresh clicked on the first one. A supplier in Surat asking about payment terms. He started typing a response, then stopped. What were the current payment terms? Had they changed with the new cash flow restrictions? He should know this. He definitely should know this.

He opened another tab, searched through policy documents, found contradictory information in two different memos, felt his heart rate spike, closed the tab.

Next email. Corporate asking for Q1 procurement reports. Due yesterday. He'd forgotten. How had he forgotten? It was on his calendar, he'd set reminders, but somehow it had slipped through the cracks like everything else was slipping through the cracks.

He started pulling data for the report, realized half the numbers were missing because three requisition orders hadn't been properly logged, felt the familiar tightness in his chest, the shortness of breath that meant he was spiraling.

Breathe. Just breathe. You can do this. You've done this job for seven years.

But that was before. Before the company started failing. Before the pressure tripled. Before Rajesh started undermining him in meetings. Before Vikram started treating procurement like an inconvenience instead of a department. Before corporate started demanding explanations for every delayed shipment and every cost overrun and every single thing that went wrong.

Before Suresh realized he wasn't actually good at his job—he'd just been good enough when the standards were lower.

At 8:30, the morning meeting started.

Suresh sat in his usual chair, hands folded in his lap to hide the trembling, listening to Meera talk about production targets and recovery plans and the need for "departmental accountability."

Departmental accountability. Translation: when things go wrong, we need someone to blame, and right now, procurement is an easy target.

"Suresh," Meera said, and his stomach dropped. "Where are we on the raw material orders for when Reactor 3 comes back online?"

"We're... processing them."

"Processing means what, exactly?"

"The orders are placed. Waiting on delivery confirmations from suppliers."

"Timelines?"

Suresh pulled up his notes, scanning frantically. "Uh... most suppliers are confirming delivery within seven to ten days of reactor restart."

"Most suppliers?"

"Three are having supply chain issues. They're... working on it."

Vikram snorted. "Working on it. Fantastic."

"Do we have backup suppliers?" Meera asked.

"We're... looking into options."

"Looking into options, or have concrete alternatives?"

Suresh felt sweat forming on his forehead. "Looking into options."

Rajesh spoke up, voice smooth and reasonable. "If I may—I've been in discussions with a supplier in Pune who can cover some of the gap. I can forward those contacts to Suresh for follow-up."

There it was. Rajesh, swooping in to save the day, making Suresh look incompetent in the process. Again.

"That would be helpful," Meera said. "Suresh, coordinate with Rajesh on this."

"Of course."

The meeting continued, but Suresh stopped listening. He sat there, nodding occasionally, while his mind screamed that he was failing, everyone could see he was failing, it was only a matter of time before they fired him, and then what? How would he find another job at forty-two with a reputation as the procurement manager who couldn't handle pressure?

After the meeting, Rajesh caught up with him in the hallway.

"Hey, I'll send you those supplier contacts."

"Thanks." Suresh tried to keep his voice neutral.

"You okay? You seem... stressed."

"I'm fine."

Rajesh studied him for a moment. "Look, I know things have been tense between us. The meeting last month where I... I was out of line. I should have talked to you directly instead of bringing up supply chain issues in front of everyone."

Was this an apology? From Rajesh? Suresh didn't trust it.

"It's fine," he said.

"It's not fine, but I appreciate you saying that. If you need help with anything—supplier negotiations, timeline management, whatever—let me know. We're supposed to be on the same team."

Rajesh walked away before Suresh could respond.

Was that genuine? Or was it Rajesh positioning himself as the helpful colleague so that when Suresh inevitably failed, Rajesh could say "I even offered to help, but..."

Suresh didn't have the energy to figure it out.

Back at his desk, he spent the next three hours trying to finish the procurement report for corporate. But the numbers wouldn't reconcile. Every time he thought he had it right, he'd find another discrepancy, another missing piece of data, another error that cascaded through the entire spreadsheet.

By noon, he'd restarted the report four times and made exactly zero progress.

His phone rang. A supplier in Mumbai, calling about a delayed payment. Suresh had forgotten about it. Again.

"Mr. Iyer, we've been very patient, but it's been forty-seven days now. Our terms are thirty days. We need payment by end of week or we'll have to suspend deliveries."

"I understand. Let me check with finance"

"You said that two weeks ago."

"I know. I'm sorry. There have been cash flow issues, but"

"Those aren't my issues, Mr. Iyer. With respect, we have our own cash flow to manage. If Apex can't pay on time, we need to know so we can plan accordingly."

"I'll get you an answer by tomorrow."

"We need payment, not answers."

The supplier hung up.

Suresh added it to his to-do list, which now had thirty-seven items, twelve of which were overdue, and twenty-three of which he'd been meaning to handle "today" for the past week.

At 2:00 PM, he realized he hadn't eaten lunch. He wasn't hungry anyway.

At 3:30, corporate called asking where the procurement report was.

"It's almost done," Suresh said. "I'll have it to you by end of day."

"It was due yesterday."

"I know. I apologize. There were some data discrepancies I needed to resolve."

"We need it today. No extensions."

After the call ended, Suresh sat there staring at his partially completed report, at the numbers that still didn't make sense, at the deadline that was impossible to meet with the level of accuracy corporate demanded.

He could submit what he had—incomplete, probably inaccurate, but at least closer to the deadline than a fully accurate version would be.

Or he could keep working and submit it late but correct.

Either way, he'd be wrong.

The thought settled over him like a weight: *Either way, I'm wrong. Every choice I make is wrong. Every decision leads to more problems. I can't do this anymore.*

His hands started shaking again. Heart racing. That familiar tightness in his chest that made it hard to breathe.

Panic attack. Another one.

Suresh stood up quickly, grabbed his phone, and walked out of his office. He needed air. Needed space. Needed to not be at his desk staring at problems he couldn't solve.

He made it to the parking lot before the full attack hit.

Chest tight like someone was sitting on it. Can't breathe. Can't think. Hands shaking so hard he dropped his phone. Vision tunneling. Heart hammering so hard he was convinced he was having a heart attack.

This is it. I'm dying. I'm dying in the Apex Chemicals parking lot because I can't handle my job.

He leaned against his car, trying to breathe, trying to calm down, trying to remember the techniques his wife had shown him from some YouTube video about managing anxiety.

Breathe in for four. Hold for four. Out for four. Hold for four.

It wasn't working. Nothing was working. Everything was

"Suresh?"

He looked up. Kavita was walking toward him, concern etched on her face.

"Are you okay?"

"I'm fine." The automatic response, even though he clearly wasn't.

Kavita came closer. "You don't look fine. You look like you're having a panic attack."

"I'm just... need some air."

"Okay. That's okay. Can I sit with you?"

Suresh nodded, not trusting his voice.

Kavita sat down on the curb next to his car, gesturing for him to do the same. He did, his legs shaking.

"Just breathe," she said quietly. "Don't try to fight it. Just let it happen and breathe through it."

They sat there for several minutes while Suresh's breathing slowly normalized, while his heart rate came down, while the world stopped feeling like it was ending.

"How long has this been happening?" Kavita asked.

"Few weeks."

"Does anyone know?"

"My wife."

"Does Meera know?"

Suresh shook his head.

"Suresh, you need to talk to someone. A doctor, HR, someone. You can't just keep pushing through this."

"If I tell HR I'm having panic attacks, they'll think I can't handle my job."

"You're having panic attacks because you can't handle your job. There's no shame in that—the job has become impossible."

"I should be able to handle it. I've been doing procurement for seven years."

"You've been doing procurement under normal circumstances for seven years. This isn't normal. The company's collapsing, corporate's breathing down everyone's necks, departments are understaffed, budgets are slashed—nobody could handle this."

"Everyone else is."

"No, they're not. They're just hiding it better. Dev's fighting battles with everyone. Vikram's destroying his relationships. Arvind's paralyzed by analysis. Ramesh is making jokes to avoid crying. We're all drowning, Suresh. You're just the first one to admit it."

Suresh looked at her. "You seem fine."

Kavita laughed, but there was no humor in it. "I cried in my car for twenty minutes yesterday because I can't fix everyone's problems and it's killing me. I'm not fine. None of us are."

They sat in silence for a moment.

"What do I do?" Suresh asked quietly.

"You talk to Meera. You tell her you're overwhelmed. You ask for help—either temporary support, or reduced responsibilities, or medical leave if you need it. But you don't just keep drowning silently."

"And if they fire me?"

"They won't fire you for being honest about struggling. And if they do, then this isn't a place worth working anyway."

Suresh wanted to believe her. But he'd seen what happened to people who admitted weakness in corporate environments. They got sidelined, overlooked, eventually pushed out.

"I'll think about it," he said.

Kavita looked at him, and he could see she knew he wouldn't. "Suresh, I can't force you to take care of yourself. But please—at least talk to your doctor. Get something for the anxiety. You can't function like this."

"Okay."

She stood up, brushed off her pants. "You're not alone in this, you know. A lot of us are barely holding it together."

After she left, Suresh sat there for another ten minutes, staring at the parking lot, at the building that had become his prison, at the car that would take him home to a family he was failing just as much as he was failing his job.

Then he stood up, picked up his phone, and went back inside.

The procurement report was still unfinished. The supplier payment was still overdue. The emails were still multiplying. The problems were still unsolvable.

But he'd try. One more time. Because what else was he supposed to do?

By 7:30 PM, Suresh submitted the report to corporate. It was incomplete. He knew it was incomplete. They'd know it was incomplete. But it was all he had.

He drove home in the dark, hands still shaking slightly on the steering wheel.

His wife had saved him dinner. His son was already in bed. The house was quiet.

"How was work?" she asked.

"Fine," he lied.

She looked at him—really looked at him—and he saw the moment she decided not to push. Not tonight.

"I'm going to make an appointment with Dr. Sharma," Suresh said quietly. "Tomorrow. I'll go."

His wife's expression shifted to something between relief and sadness. "Okay. That's good. That's a good step."

Suresh nodded, too exhausted to say anything else.

He went to bed at 9:00 PM but didn't sleep until after midnight, his mind cycling through tomorrow's problems, next week's deadlines, next month's impossibilities.

And somewhere in the dark, the thought crept in that he'd been pushing away for weeks:

What if I just... quit?

What if he walked away? Found something easier, something less stressful, something that didn't make him have panic attacks in parking lots?

But then what? Take a pay cut they couldn't afford? Start over at forty-two in a new industry? Admit defeat?

The thoughts spiraled until exhaustion finally dragged him under into restless sleep filled with dreams about spreadsheets that never balanced and emails that multiplied faster than he could read them and meetings where everyone was shouting but he couldn't understand what they were saying.

He woke up at 4:47 AM, heart already racing, to start it all over again.

Because that's what you did.

You kept going.

Even when you couldn't.

Even when it was breaking you.

Even when the cost of caring about doing your job well was higher than you could afford to pay.

You kept going.

Until you couldn't anymore.

9

THE ARCHITECT OF UNITY

Priya Nair learned to build bridges when her parents divorced.

She was fourteen, caught between a mother who wouldn't speak to a father who wouldn't apologize, both of them using her as a messenger because direct communication had become impossible. Every weekend was a negotiation. Every holiday was a battle. Every decision about her life required her to translate between two people who'd once loved each other but now couldn't occupy the same room.

So Priya became a translator. A mediator. A person who could see both sides, validate both perspectives, and somehow find the narrow path between them where everyone could move forward even if nobody got exactly what they wanted.

The final act hovers, waiting to begin.

It was exhausting. But it worked.

Twenty-three years later, she was Director of Operations Integration at Apex Chemicals, and she was about to attempt the most ambitious mediation of her career: getting nine dysfunctional leaders to actually work together before the company collapsed completely.

She'd been planning this for three weeks. Not officially—she didn't have the authority to call an emergency leadership summit. But she had something more useful than authority: she had relationships.

Meera trusted her. Kavita considered her a friend. Arvind respected her judgment. Even Vikram listened to her occasionally, probably because she was one of the few people who didn't flinch when he started shouting.

And she'd used all of those relationships to orchestrate what would either save Apex Chemicals or prove that some things were too broken to fix.

The email had gone out three days ago:

LEADERSHIP ALIGNMENT SESSIONSaturday, March 15th, 8:00 AM - 4:00 PMRetreat Center, Anand

Mandatory attendance. No phones. No laptops. No excuses.

We're going to fix this, or we're going to admit we can't. But we're not leaving until we have a real plan.

She'd expected pushback. She got it.

Vikram: **I have actual work to do. We don't have time for corporate trust falls.**

Rajesh: **Who authorized this? What's the budget? Who's facilitating?**

Dev: **Finally. Someone willing to actually DO something.**

Ramesh: **Will there be snacks? I'm not sitting through 8 hours without snacks.**

Suresh: **I... okay. I'll be there.**

But Meera had backed her. Sent a follow-up email making it clear this wasn't optional. Corporate had signed off, probably because they were desperate enough to try anything.

Now it was Saturday morning, 7:47 AM, and Priya stood in the conference room of a retreat center thirty kilometers outside Nadiad, arranging chairs in a circle instead of around a table.

No table. That was deliberate. Tables were barriers. Tables let people hide behind laptops and papers. Tables created hierarchy

—who sat at the head, who sat at the sides, who got pushed to the corners.

A circle meant everyone was equal. Everyone was exposed. Everyone had to actually look at each other.

The room was simple. White walls, large windows overlooking a garden, wooden floors. She'd chosen this place specifically because it didn't look like Apex. Didn't smell like chemicals and stress. Didn't carry the weight of all their failures.

Fresh start. Neutral ground.

Arvind arrived first, exactly thirteen minutes early, leather notebook under his arm.

"No laptops," Priya reminded him.

"It's a notebook. Paper."

"I know. You're fine."

He surveyed the room, the circle of chairs, and nodded slowly. "Interesting setup."

"You think it'll work?"

"I think it's a well-designed intervention. Whether it works depends on whether people want it to work."

"What do you think?"

Arvind sat down, opened his notebook to a fresh page. "I think we're nine people who've forgotten we're supposed to be on the same team. But I also think some of us are invested in being right more than being successful. Those two things are hard to reconcile."

Kavita arrived next, carrying a bag of homemade snacks—samosas and mathri and something that smelled like cardamom. "I know you said you'd provide food, but I made these anyway."

"Ramesh will love you forever."

"Ramesh already loves everyone. It's his superpower and his defense mechanism."

They arranged the snacks on a side table. More people filtered in. Dev arrived looking cautiously optimistic. Meera arrived looking exhausted. Vikram arrived radiating hostility. Rajesh arrived checking his phone until Priya literally took it from him and put it in a basket by the door.

"You'll get it back at 4:00 PM."

"What if there's an emergency?"

"Then someone will find you. Eight hours without your phone won't kill you."

Ramesh wandered in, immediately found the snacks, and started eating while making conversation with Kavita about her daughter's exam results. Normal human interaction, like they weren't in the middle of a corporate crisis.

Suresh arrived last, looking worse than Priya had ever seen him. Dark circles under his eyes, hands shaking slightly when he set down his bag. She made a mental note to check in with him privately during breaks.

At 8:00 exactly, everyone was seated in the circle.

Nine people. Nine completely different approaches to leadership. Nine conflicting visions of how to save—or at least manage—a dying company.

Priya stood in the center of the circle.

"Thank you all for coming. I know you have better things to do on a Saturday morning—"

"That's an understatement," Vikram muttered.

"—but we're here because Apex Chemicals is failing, and we're failing it. We're smart people. We're experienced. We care about this place. But we can't agree on anything, we don't trust each other, and we're spending more energy fighting each other than fighting the actual problems."

She paused, looking at each of them.

"Today, we're going to change that. Not through speeches or presentations or anyone telling anyone else what to do. Through actual conversation. Through listening—really listening—to perspectives we usually dismiss. Through finding common ground even when we think there isn't any."

"And if we can't?" Vikram asked.

"Then we'll have our answer about whether this leadership team is capable of saving this company. And we can all start planning our exits accordingly."

The bluntness landed. Good.

"Here's how this works," Priya continued. "We're going to go through three sessions. Session one: What's actually true? We're going to align on the reality of our situation without spin, without blame, without politics. Session two: What does each of us actually want? Not what we say we want in meetings—what we genuinely want for ourselves, for this company, for our teams. Session three: What can we actually do? Not perfect solutions, not five-year plans—practical actions we can take starting Monday."

She sat down in her chair, becoming part of the circle.

"First rule: No interrupting. When someone's talking, everyone else listens. Second rule: No defensiveness. If someone criticizes your department or your decisions, you can respond, but not with excuses—with acknowledgment of what's true in what they're saying. Third rule: No phones, no side conversations, no checking out mentally. We're here. We're present. We're doing this."

"And if someone breaks the rules?" Rajesh asked.

"I'll call it out. And if I break the rules, any of you can call me out. We're all accountable. Including me."

She pulled out a small stack of index cards. "We're going to start with a simple exercise. I'm going to hand each of you a card. On it, write one sentence: 'The biggest problem at Apex is...' and finish that sentence. Honest answer. Not what you think you're supposed to say—what you actually believe is the core problem."

Cards went around the circle. Pens came out. People wrote.

After two minutes, Priya collected the cards, shuffled them, and read them aloud:

"The biggest problem at Apex is that we have outdated systems and refuse to modernize." - Obviously Dev.

"The biggest problem at Apex is that we tolerate mediocrity and call it compassion." - Definitely Vikram.

"The biggest problem at Apex is that we've lost sight of the human beings behind the production numbers." - Kavita, without question.

"The biggest problem at Apex is that we make decisions based on politics instead of data." - Arvind.

"The biggest problem at Apex is that nobody trusts anyone else."- Small, careful handwriting. Unidentifiable. It could have come from any of them. Perhaps that was the point.

"The biggest problem at Apex is that we're reactive instead of strategic." - Probably Rajesh.

"The biggest problem at Apex is that we use humor to avoid dealing with real issues." - Ramesh. Self-aware, at least.

"The biggest problem at Apex is that we're drowning and pretending we're swimming." - Suresh. Heartbreaking.

"The biggest problem at Apex is that we have nine leaders and zero leadership." - Meera. Brutal.

Silence after that last one.

"Show of hands," Priya said. "How many of you think all nine of these statements are at least partially true?"

Every hand went up. Slowly, reluctantly, but they all went up.

"Good. We agree on something. We're a disaster. Now let's figure out what kind of disaster, and whether it's fixable."

She pointed to the first card. "Dev, talk to us about modernization. Not why we should do it—we've heard that. Tell us why you think we're refusing."

Dev shifted in his seat. "Because change is scary. Because it requires upfront investment when we're cash-strapped. Because it might fail, and then whoever championed it gets blamed. Because it's easier to keep doing what we've always done, even if it's slowly killing us."

"Is that what you think we're doing?" Meera asked. "Choosing easy over effective?"

"I think... I think some of you are. Not maliciously. But yes."

"And I think you're confusing 'refusing to modernize' with 'refusing to bet the company on unproven tech during a crisis,'" Arvind said calmly.

"It's not unproven—"

"No interrupting," Priya reminded them. "Arvind, finish your thought."

"It's not that we don't see the value in automation. It's that the timing is terrible, the risk is high, and you're presenting it like anyone who disagrees is an idiot stuck in the past. That's not collaboration. That's condescension."

Dev's jaw tightened, but he nodded. "Fair."

Priya pointed to Vikram's card. "Vikram. Mediocrity and compassion. Explain."

Vikram leaned back. "We have people who can't do their jobs. Everyone knows it. But instead of dealing with it, we make excuses. 'They're trying their best.' 'They're dealing with personal issues.' 'We need to be understanding.' Meanwhile, good workers are carrying dead weight and burning out."

Kavita spoke up. "And you think the solution is to just fire people and bring in new ones, like humans are interchangeable parts."

"I think the solution is to have standards and enforce them. Yes."

"Even when those standards are unreasonable? Even when we've created an environment so toxic that people can't succeed?"

"Standards aren't toxic. Accountability isn't toxic."

"Cruelty is toxic. And you've crossed that line repeatedly."

The tension spiked. Priya held up a hand.

"Both of you—acknowledge what's true in what the other person is saying. Vikram first."

Vikram was quiet for a long moment. Then: "It's true that I'm harsh. It's true that my approach has driven people away. It's true that I sometimes conflate 'tough' with 'effective' when they're not the same thing."

Kavita looked surprised by the admission.

"Now you," Priya said to Kavita.

"It's true that we have performance issues we're not addressing. It's true that being kind doesn't automatically make someone effective. It's true that I sometimes prioritize feelings over results in ways that aren't sustainable."

The air in the room shifted slightly. Not agreement, exactly. But acknowledgment. Space.

Priya continued through the cards, forcing each person to explain their perspective and then forcing everyone else to find the truth in it.

Rajesh admitting that politics sometimes drove his decisions more than data.

Ramesh admitting that he used humor to avoid uncomfortable truths.

Suresh admitting that he was drowning and had been for months.

Meera admitting that she'd been so focused on managing crises that she'd lost sight of actual leadership.

Arvind admitting that his patience was sometimes just paralysis in disguise.

By 11:30, they were all exhausted. Emotionally raw. But something had shifted.

They weren't enemies anymore. Just nine deeply flawed people trying to save something that mattered, each one broken in their own way, each one right about some things and catastrophically wrong about others.

Priya called a break. "Thirty minutes. Stretch. Eat. Think."

People dispersed. Priya found Suresh standing by the windows, staring out at the garden.

"You okay?" she asked quietly.

"No. But I said it out loud, so that's something."

"You need more than this session. You know that, right?"

"I have a doctor's appointment on Monday."

"Good. That's good." She paused. "For what it's worth, you're not weak for struggling. You're human for acknowledging it."

Suresh nodded but didn't respond.

At noon, they reconvened for session two: What do we actually want?

This was harder. Scarier. Required vulnerability most of them weren't used to.

"I want the plant to survive," Meera said. "But more than that, I want to not feel like I'm the only one carrying the weight of whether it does."

"I want respect," Vikram said. "I want people to recognize that standards matter, even if they don't like how I enforce them."

"I want people to care about each other," Kavita said. "I want us to remember we're dealing with humans, not machines."

"I want permission to make the changes I know we need," Dev said. "Without having to fight for every inch of progress."

"I want data to matter," Arvind said. "I want us to make decisions based on evidence instead of whoever argues loudest."

"I want to influence outcomes," Rajesh said carefully. "I want to matter. I want my voice to count."

"I want everyone to lighten up," Ramesh said. "I want us to remember that work is important but it's not everything."

"I want to not feel like I'm failing all the time," Suresh said quietly.

"I want us to function as a team," Priya said. "I want to believe that nine smart people can be more than the sum of their dysfunctions."

Another silence. Longer this time.

"You know what's interesting?" Arvind said slowly. "None of those wants are actually contradictory. They're just... different facets of the same thing. We all want to matter. We all want our approach to be valued. We all want to succeed."

"And we've been treating it like a competition instead of a collaboration," Kavita added.

"Because we don't trust each other," Rajesh said. "I assume Kavita's going to be too soft. Kavita assumes I'm going to be too political. Vikram assumes everyone's incompetent. Dev assumes everyone's backwards. We've all decided what everyone else is before we actually listen."

The room went quiet.

"So how do we fix that?" Meera asked.

"We start by acknowledging we're all partially right and partially wrong," Priya said. "And then we build something that incorporates everyone's strengths instead of just fighting over whose weakness matters more."

Session three started at 1:30 PM: What can we actually do?

This was the practical part. The translation of insight into action.

Priya handed out fresh index cards. "Three actions. Specific. Measurable. Starting Monday. What's one thing you personally will do differently? What's one thing you need from this team? What's one thing we should do collectively?"

They wrote. Shared. Debated.

By 3:00 PM, they had something that almost resembled a plan:

IMMEDIATE ACTIONS:

• **Weekly leadership check-ins** - 30 minutes, every Monday, just to align and surface issues before they explode

• **Cross-department shadowing** - Each leader spends 4 hours monthly in another department to understand their reality

• **Decision framework** - Clear criteria for who makes what decisions, how we disagree productively, when we escalate to the group

• **Support for Suresh** - Temporary help for procurement, explicit permission to delegate, mandatory mental health resources

• **Pilot program for automation** - Small scale, Reactor 6, Dev leads but Arvind oversees risk assessment

• **Performance standards review** - Vikram and Kavita work together to define fair standards that balance accountability and humanity

• **Communication training** - All of them, including Vikram, including Rajesh, no exceptions

• **Monthly pulse checks** - Anonymous feedback from floor workers about leadership effectiveness

• **Quarterly strategic reviews** - Step back from crisis management long enough to actually plan

It wasn't perfect. It wasn't comprehensive. But it was real.

And more importantly, they'd built it together.

At 3:45, Priya stood up. "Last thing. We're going around the circle one more time. One sentence. 'I commit to...' Whatever you're personally committing to do differently starting Monday. Not what you hope to do. What you will do."

They went around:

Meera: "I commit to delegating more and trusting people to handle things instead of trying to control everything."

Arvind: "I commit to making decisions with imperfect information instead of waiting for perfect data."

Kavita: "I commit to balancing empathy with accountability instead of letting compassion excuse poor performance."

Vikram: "I commit to... being less of atyrant. More specifically, to giving feedback that improves people instead of just breaking them."

Dev: "I commit to listening to concerns about my ideas instead of dismissing everyone who questions them as backwards."

Rajesh: "I commit to being direct instead of political when something needs to be addressed."

Ramesh: "I commit to using humor to build us up instead of helping us avoid hard truths."

Suresh: "I commit to asking for help before I break completely."

Priya: "I commit to holding all of us accountable to what we said today, even when it's uncomfortable."

At 4:00 PM exactly, Priya handed back phones.

Nobody checked them immediately. They just sat there, nine people who'd spent eight hours being more honest than they'd been in months.

"Will this actually work?" Vikram asked finally.

"I don't know," Priya admitted. "We might walk back into Apex on Monday and fall into all the same patterns. But at least now we know we have a choice. We can keep being nine separate disasters, or we can try being one functional team."

"That's very optimistic," Rajesh said.

"I prefer 'aggressively hopeful.'"

They started packing up. Conversations continued in smaller groups. Kavita and Vikram actually talking—not arguing, talking—about how to define performance standards. Dev and Arvind discussing risk frameworks for the automation pilot. Suresh accepting Meera's offer to bring in temporary procurement support.

Not perfect. Not solved. But different.

As people left, Meera pulled Priya aside.

"This was good. Really good. I don't know if it'll be enough, but... thank you."

"Don't thank me yet. Making people talk is easy. Making change stick is hard."

"Still. You did something none of us could do alone."

After everyone left, Priya sat alone in the empty conference room for a few minutes.

Nine chairs in a circle. Crumpled index cards. Half-eaten snacks.

Evidence of something. Maybe progress. Maybe just a brief moment of clarity before they all fell back into their patterns.

She pulled out her phone and saw seventeen missed messages. Mostly work stuff. One from her partner asking how it went.

She typed back: **We'll see. Ask me again in a month.**

Because that was the truth. Today had been important. Maybe even transformative.

But transformation didn't happen in a single eight-hour session.

It happened in a thousand small choices over weeks and months, when the inspiration faded and the work got hard and it would be so much easier to just go back to being right instead of being effective.

The question wasn't whether they could work together for one day.

It was whether they'd choose to keep working together when they didn't have to anymore.

Priya turned off the lights and locked the door behind her, carrying that question with her into the uncertain future.

10

SABOTAGE IN SILENCE

The alarm started screaming at 2:47 AM.

Ravi Malhotra, night shift supervisor, was doing his rounds near Reactor Hall C when every screen on the monitoring wall turned red simultaneously. Not one system failing—all of them. Temperature spikes across multiple lines. Pressure irregularities. Flow rate disruptions.

And Reactor 5—the stable one, the one that never had problems—showing readings that made no sense.

He grabbed his radio. "Control room, this is Malhotra. We have multiple critical alerts. Reactor 5 showing—" He looked at the screen again, not believing what he was seeing. "—showing coolant system failure and internal temperature at 187 degrees. That's not possible."

"Confirmed," the control room operator responded, voice tight. "Initiating emergency shutdown protocol."

But the shutdown wasn't working.

The system that should have automatically cut feeds, dumped pressure, and brought the reactor to safe idle—it wasn't responding.

Manual override. They had to do it manually.

Ravi ran toward Reactor 5, shouting into his radio for the emergency response team. Other operators were already moving, years of safety drills overriding panic.

But something was wrong. More wrong than just a malfunction.

The access panel to the manual shutdown controls was open. Hanging open. Like someone had already been there.

And the override mechanism—the physical lever that would cut all power to the reactor regardless of what the computer systems said—was missing.

Not broken. Missing. As in removed. As in taken.

"Control room, we have a problem. Manual override is gone. Someone removed it."

Silence on the radio for three seconds that felt like hours.

Then: "Say again?"

"The physical override lever. It's not here. Someone took it."

"That's... that's not possible. It's bolted down, it requires—"

"I'm looking at empty bolt holes. It's gone."

Around him, alarms screamed. Reactor 5's temperature continued climbing. 192 degrees. 197 degrees. At 215 degrees, they'd have a cascade failure. At 230 degrees, they'd have an explosion.

They had maybe eight minutes.

By 3:15 AM, the emergency team had managed to manually shut off feed lines using backup access points never designed to be primary controls. By 3:32 AM, they'd vented enough pressure to stabilize the reactor. By 3:51 AM, Reactor 5 was in safe shutdown, the building was evacuated as a precaution, and Ravi was standing in the parking lot watching police cars arrive.

Because this wasn't an accident. This wasn't equipment failure or operator error.

This was sabotage.

Meera got the call at 4:03 AM. She was at the plant by 4:37.

The main conference room had become an emergency command center. Ravi Malhotra looking exhausted and shaken. Three police officers. A government safety inspector who'd been woken up and was clearly not happy about it. The lead engineer examining photos of the missing override mechanism on a tablet.

"Walk me through it," Meera said.

Ravi repeated the timeline. The simultaneous alarms. The impossible readings. The missing override lever.

"Could it have been taken for maintenance?" one of the police officers asked.

The lead engineer—Prakash Reddy—shook his head. "No. That part never gets removed. It's literally the last-resort safety mechanism. The thing you use when everything else fails. You don't take it off for maintenance or cleaning or anything. And even if you did, you'd lock out the reactor completely until it was replaced. You wouldn't leave the reactor operational with no emergency shutoff."

"Who has access to that area?" the safety inspector asked.

"During night shift? Operators, supervisors, maintenance crew, engineering. Maybe thirty people total."

"And during day shift?"

"Closer to a hundred. But this happened at night."

Meera's phone was vibrating nonstop. The rest of the leadership team finding out. Corporate demanding explanations. She ignored them for now.

"Cameras?" she asked.

"We're pulling footage," the senior police officer said. "But your security system is... limited. Cameras only cover entry points and main corridors. Not individual reactor stations."

Of course not. Because that upgrade had been "deferred" three budgets in a row.

The door opened. Arvind walked in, fully dressed despite the hour, notebook already in hand.

"I heard," was all he said, taking a seat and immediately starting to document everything being discussed.

Gradually, the rest arrived. Kavita in sweatpants and a company polo, hair pulled back hastily. Vikram in workout clothes, looking simultaneously furious and energized by the crisis. Rajesh dressed like he'd been expecting this, which made Meera wonder how he'd gotten here so fast and so prepared. Dev in pajama pants and an MIT sweatshirt. Ramesh looking uncharacteristically serious. Even Suresh showed up, though he looked like he might vomit.

Priya was the last to arrive, and she immediately started organizing—getting coffee made, setting up a proper timeline on the whiteboard, creating information flow structure.

At 6:00 AM, as the sun was coming up, they gathered for a formal briefing.

"Here's what we know," Meera said. "Reactor 5 had a near-catastrophic failure overnight that was prevented by quick action from our night crew. Investigation revealed that the manual emergency override mechanism had been deliberately removed. This was not an accident. This was sabotage."

The word landed like a bomb.

"The police are investigating. The government safety inspector is investigating. We're investigating. But I need to be very clear about something: this plant does not operate until we know what happened, who did it, and why. As of now, we're in complete shutdown except for essential safety systems."

"For how long?" Vikram demanded.

"Until we have answers."

"That could be days. Weeks. We'll lose every remaining client."

"And if we have a saboteur operating freely in this facility and someone gets killed, we'll lose a lot more than clients."

The room was silent.

"Everyone here is a suspect," the senior police officer said bluntly. "Everyone who had access to that facility in the past week. That includes all of you."

Rajesh laughed—not because it was funny, but because it was absurd. "You think one of us sabotaged our own plant?"

"I think someone did. And until we know who and why, everyone's a possibility."

"This is ridiculous," Vikram said. "We should be focusing on the floor workers. Someone with a grudge, someone who got disciplined or fired—"

"Like the three people you drove to quit last month?" Kavita cut in.

"Are you seriously suggesting this is my fault?"

"I'm suggesting that when you treat people like garbage, they stop caring about the company's wellbeing."

"So you think what—one of them came back in the middle of the night, somehow got past security, removed a safety mechanism, and tried to blow up the plant? That's your theory?"

"It's more plausible than the idea that one of us did it!"

The argument escalated. Meera tried to regain control. The police officer threatened to clear the room. Priya stepped between Vikram and Kavita physically.

Arvind sat quietly, writing in his notebook, observing everything.

Dev noticed. "You're very calm about this."

Arvind looked up. "I'm documenting patterns. Someone's behavior right now will tell us something. Possibly who did this. Possibly who benefits from it."

"You think someone here did it," Dev said flatly.

"I think someone with intimate knowledge of this plant's systems did it. The override lever isn't just sitting there accessible. You need to know where it is, how it's secured, what removing it would accomplish. That's inside knowledge."

"Inside knowledge that hundreds of people have," Rajesh pointed out.

"Yes. But only nine people benefit from the plant failing completely."

Everyone went silent.

"What are you implying?" Meera asked carefully.

"I'm not implying anything. I'm stating a fact: if this plant closes, most workers lose their jobs. Most suppliers lose a client. Most of us lose our positions. But someone in this room might benefit from failure. Someone who's positioned themselves to land elsewhere. Someone who's been making deals. Someone who's been setting up their next move."

All eyes turned to Rajesh.

"You're accusing me?" Rajesh's voice was dangerously quiet.

"I'm observing that you've been having a lot of private supplier meetings lately. That you're frequently on calls with corporate. That you've been positioning yourself as the bridge between this facility and headquarters. And that if this plant closes, you're the most likely to land a corporate role elsewhere."

"That's insane. Why would I sabotage the place that employs me?"

"Because it's failing anyway. Because you could accelerate the timeline, blame it on management incompetence, and emerge as the person who tried to save it but couldn't because everyone else was dysfunctional."

"This is—"

"Let him finish," Meera said.

Arvind continued, voice calm and analytical. "I'm not saying you did it. I'm saying you have motive. But so does Vikram—

proving that aggressive management was necessary by forcing a crisis that validates his approach. So does Dev—creating a disaster that can only be fixed by automation, proving his point. So does Kavita—if this place is toxic enough, maybe closure is the merciful option. So do I—letting things fail catastrophically to prove that analysis and caution were correct."

He closed his notebook.

"We all have motives. The question is who had opportunity and follow-through."

The police officer stepped forward. "We'll be conducting individual interviews with each of you. Starting now. Nobody leaves the facility until we're done."

The interviews took hours.

Each person was taken to a separate room. Asked about their whereabouts last night. Their knowledge of the override system. Their relationships with floor workers. Their grievances with management. Their future plans.

Meera went first. She'd been home, asleep. Her husband confirmed it. She had no particular knowledge of Reactor 5's override system beyond general awareness. She was stressed, yes. Overwhelmed, yes. But she had no motive to destroy what she'd been working to save.

Arvind went second. He'd also been home. Alone. No alibi. He had extensive knowledge of all systems—he'd documented everything, including safety mechanisms. Motive? He claimed none, but his constant observation and documentation of dysfunction could be interpreted as someone planning to write a case study on failure.

Kavita went third. Home with her family. Verifiable alibi. Limited technical knowledge of the specific override system. Motive? Maybe, if you believed someone might sabotage the plant to save workers from a toxic environment.

Vikram went fourth. At the gym, then home. Partial alibi—the gym's 24-hour security could confirm his entry and exit. Substantial technical knowledge. Strong motive if you believed he wanted to prove that tough management was necessary by creating a crisis.

Dev went fifth. Home, but couldn't sleep, had been working on his automation proposal until 2:00 AM. Computer logs could potentially confirm. Deep technical knowledge. Clear motive: prove that human operators were unreliable and automation was necessary.

Rajesh went sixth. "Working late at home" on supplier contracts. No alibi. Significant knowledge of plant systems despite not being operations-focused. Motive: as Arvind had pointed out, he was positioned to benefit from failure.

Ramesh went seventh. Home with his family, verifiable alibi. Limited technical knowledge—he was HR and culture focused. Motive? None apparent, unless you thought his jokes were covering something darker.

Suresh went eighth. Home, but his wife said he'd gotten up around 2:00 AM, couldn't sleep, went for a drive. No clear alibi for the exact time of the incident. Moderate technical knowledge. Motive? Maybe. A stressed person at breaking point might do irrational things.

Priya went last. Home, alone, asleep. No alibi. Moderate technical knowledge. Motive? The least obvious—she'd just spent a full day trying to unite the team. Why sabotage that?

By noon, they had no clear suspect. Just nine people with varying levels of motive, opportunity, and knowledge.

And a plant that was completely shut down while investigators examined every inch of Reactor 5 and interviewed night shift workers.

At 2:00 PM, a discovery.

One of the night shift operators—a young man named Kiran—remembered something. Around 1:30 AM, during his rounds, he'd seen someone near Reactor 5 who shouldn't have been there. But it was dark, the figure was in shadow, and Kiran had assumed it was maintenance or engineering.

"Can you describe them?"

"Not really. Average height. Wearing a company jacket and hard hat. I only saw them for a second."

"Male or female?"

"I... I don't know. I didn't get a good look."

Dead end. But at least confirmation that someone had been there who didn't belong.

At 3:30 PM, security footage review found something interesting.

At 1:17 AM, someone had entered the facility through the east loading dock entrance—an area with minimal camera coverage. The footage was grainy, showing only a silhouette in company safety gear.

But the security log showed no authorized entry at that time.

Someone with access credentials had come in off-hours without authorization.

"Can we trace whose credentials were used?" Meera asked.

The security manager looked uncomfortable. "The system... it's old. It logs entries but not which specific credential card. Just that a valid card was used."

Of course. Another deferred upgrade.

They pulled records of who had access credentials. Over three hundred people. Including all nine of them.

At 6:00 PM, exhausted and no closer to answers, they reconvened.

"Where are we?" Meera asked the police officer.

"Nowhere definitive. We have evidence of deliberate sabotage. We have a time frame. We have a list of people with access and knowledge. But we don't have a clear suspect."

"How long until we can reopen?"

"That's not my call. That's the safety inspector's call."

The inspector spoke up. "Minimum three days. We need to inspect every safety system in this facility. If one was compromised, others might be too. And frankly, until you know who did this and why, I'm not comfortable authorizing restart."

"Three days," Vikram said. "Minimum. We're done. The clients will be gone."

"Better than the alternative," Kavita said quietly.

"Which is what?"

"Someone dies."

Nobody argued with that.

As people started to leave, Arvind approached Meera privately.

"I think we're asking the wrong question," he said.

"Which is?"

"We're asking who did this. We should be asking who benefits from making us ask that question."

Meera frowned. "Meaning?"

"Meaning maybe the sabotage isn't about destroying the plant. Maybe it's about destroying us. Making us suspect each other. Accelerating the distrust that was already fracturing this leadership team."

"That's... that's pretty elaborate."

"Is it? We just spent eight hours yesterday trying to build unity. And now we're spending eight hours today suspecting each other of sabotage. Someone might want us divided. Might benefit from us turning on each other."

"Who?"

Arvind looked at her steadily. "I don't know. But I think we should find out before we destroy each other doing the saboteur's work for them."

He walked away, leaving Meera with that thought.

That night, unable to sleep, she pulled out her phone and started going through everything that had happened in the past month. Every conflict. Every decision. Every moment where someone had pushed the team toward division instead of unity.

And slowly, a pattern emerged.

Not definitive. Not conclusive. But enough to make her wonder.

Enough to make her very, very worried about what Monday would bring.

Because if Arvind was right—if this was about dividing them rather than destroying the plant—then the real sabotage wasn't the missing override lever.

It was what that missing lever made them do to each other.

And they'd fallen for it completely.

PART IV

UNITY OR RUIN

11

THE FAULT IN AUTHORITY

The emergency meeting started at 8:00 AM Monday morning in the main conference room, but nobody was really there.

Physically present, yes. Nine bodies in chairs around a table. But mentally, emotionally, they were scattered across a landscape of suspicion, fear, and barely controlled panic.

The plant had been shut down for three days. Corporate had called seventeen times. Two more clients had sent termination notices. The media had picked up the story—"Chemical Plant Sabotage Raises Safety Concerns"—and suddenly Apex Chemicals was national news for all the wrong reasons.

New stories rise where old ones yield.

And they still didn't know who did it.

Meera stood at the head of the table, looking like she'd aged five years in three days. Dark circles under her eyes. Hair pulled back in a hasty ponytail. A coffee cup she'd been refilling every thirty minutes since 5:00 AM.

"The safety inspector cleared us to restart operations this morning," she began. "Every system has been checked. Additional security protocols are in place. But before we restart, we need to address what happened. Because if we can't trust each other, none of these matters."

"Trust?" Vikram laughed, sharp and bitter. "Trust is gone. Someone in this building tried to blow up a reactor. Until we know who, how are we supposed to trust anyone?"

"The police investigation is ongoing," Rajesh said carefully. "Maybe we should wait for official conclusions before we start accusing—"

"Accusing who?" Vikram cut in. "You? Because Arvind made a pretty compelling case that you're the one with the most to gain from this place failing."

"I made observations," Arvind said calmly. "I didn't accuse anyone specifically."

"You accused everyone generally, which is somehow worse."

"I stated that we all have potential motives. That's just factual analysis."

"It's paranoid speculation dressed up as logic."

Meera held up her hand. "Enough. We're not here to—"

"No," Kavita interrupted, her voice tight with something between anger and heartbreak. "Let's actually do this. Let's say what we're all thinking instead of dancing around it."

She stood up, facing the table.

"Vikram thinks I did it to prove the environment was toxic. Dev thinks it was Vikram trying to create a crisis that validates his aggressive approach. Rajesh thinks it was Dev trying to prove automation is necessary. Arvind suspects Rajesh because of his corporate connections. I suspect Suresh because he was literally having a breakdown and people do irrational things when they break. Suresh probably suspects all of us because we've been making his life hell. Ramesh doesn't know who to suspect because he's too busy making jokes to process actual emotion. And Priya—"

She looked at Priya, who was sitting very still.

"—Priya just spent an entire day getting us to open up and trust each other, which makes her either the most genuine person here or the most manipulative, depending on whether Saturday was about unity or intelligence gathering."

The room went dead silent.

Priya's face was carefully neutral, but something flickered in her eyes. Pain, maybe. Or recognition that Kavita had just articulated everyone's unspoken fear.

"Is that really what you think?" Priya asked quietly. "That I orchestrated a team-building session as a cover for sabotage?"

"I don't know what I think anymore," Kavita said, sitting back down. "That's the problem. Three days ago, I thought we'd turned a corner. Now I'm questioning every conversation, every interaction, wondering who's genuine and who's playing us."

Dev spoke up. "The sabotage happened Saturday night, right after our session. That timing feels deliberate."

"What are you suggesting?" Priya's voice had an edge now.

"I'm suggesting someone wanted to undo what we built. Either someone in this room who didn't like the unity direction, or someone outside who felt threatened by it."

"Outside?" Meera frowned. "You think a floor worker did this?"

"I think we're so focused on suspecting each other that we're ignoring other possibilities."

Ramesh, who'd been uncharacteristically quiet, finally spoke. "What if it wasn't about the plant at all?"

Everyone turned to look at him.

"What do you mean?" Arvind asked.

"I mean, what if this wasn't about destroying equipment or causing an explosion? What if it was about doing exactly what it's doing right now—destroying us."

He gestured around the table.

"Three days ago, we actually agreed on something. We committed to working together. And now? Now we're right back to suspecting and attacking and fracturing. Maybe that was the goal. Maybe someone wanted to prove that we can't work together. That we're too broken to save this place."

"But who benefits from that?" Vikram demanded.

"Corporate," Suresh said quietly. It was the first thing he'd said all meeting. "If they can prove that leadership is dysfunctional beyond repair, they have justification to shut us down and relocate operations. Clean narrative. No pushback."

"You think corporate sabotaged their own facility?" Rajesh's voice dripped with skepticism.

"I think someone who wants this place closed might have. And corporate's been looking for an excuse."

"That's a conspiracy theory," Vikram said.

"Is it?" Suresh looked around the table. "We're a failing plant in a competitive market. Corporate could cut their losses, shift production to Bangalore where costs are lower, and blame it on 'unforeseen safety incidents and management dysfunction.' We're giving them exactly the story they need."

Meera's phone buzzed. She glanced at it and her face went pale.

"Corporate just sent an email. Emergency board meeting. Thursday. We're required to present a full report on the incident, our investigation findings, and our plan for 'organizational restructuring.'"

"Restructuring," Dev repeated. "That's corporate speak for 'we're shutting you down.'"

"We don't know that—"

"Yes, we do. This is what it looks like. They're building a case."

The despair in the room was palpable. They'd been fighting to save the plant for months, and now, whether or not they'd done the sabotage themselves, it was working as sabotage perfectly.

Priya stood up. "Stop."

Her voice cut through the spiral.

"Just stop. All of you. Do you hear yourselves? We're doing exactly what someone wants—falling apart, blaming each other, giving up. And I don't know if that someone is in this room or outside it or sitting in a corporate office in Bangalore, but I know we're playing right into it."

"What do you suggest?" Meera asked tiredly.

"I suggest we work backwards. Not from 'who did it' but from 'what actually happened.' Facts. Timeline. Evidence. Like Arvind would do. And then we figure out what we do with that information."

Arvind nodded slowly. "Agreed. Let's start with what we know for certain, not what we suspect."

He opened his leather notebook to pages he'd filled over the past three days.

"Saturday: Leadership session ends at 4:00 PM. Everyone leaves. Facility operates normally through evening shift. Saturday night:

Evening shift ends at 11:00 PM. Night shift begins. At 1:17 AM, someone enters through east loading dock using valid credentials. At 1:30 AM, operator Kiran sees someone near Reactor 5 who shouldn't be there. At 2:47 AM, alarms trigger. Emergency response finds override mechanism missing."

He looked up.

"Key questions: Who entered at 1:17 AM? Why remove the override rather than actually causing immediate damage? Why Reactor 5 specifically?"

"Reactor 5 is the most stable unit," the lead engineer Prakash Reddy said. He'd been sitting quietly in the corner, having been called in as technical consultant. "If you wanted to actually cause an explosion, you'd target Reactor 3 or 4—they're already stressed. Reactor 5 is overbuilt, redundant systems, hardest to actually destroy."

"So someone chose the reactor least likely to actually explode," Kavita said slowly. "That's... that's weird, right?"

"Unless causing an explosion wasn't the goal," Arvind said.

"Then what was?"

"Exactly what happened. An emergency. An investigation. A shutdown. Us, right here, suspecting each other."

Dev leaned forward. "The credentials. Can we narrow down whose might have been used?"

"Three hundred people have access credentials," Meera said. "That's not narrowing."

"But how many people have credentials AND detailed knowledge of where the override mechanism is AND motive to disrupt without destroying?"

"Still dozens, probably."

Rajesh spoke up. "What about the timing? Specifically, Saturday night, hours after our session. That's either coincidence or deliberate."

"Not coincidence," Arvind said firmly. "The timing is the message. 'You tried to come together. I'm showing you why that won't work.'"

"But who would—" Kavita started, then stopped. "Wait."

Everyone looked at her.

"What?" Meera asked.

"There's someone we haven't talked about. Someone who wasn't at the leadership session. Someone who's been cynical about every positive change, who undermines morale, who's always in the background watching."

"Who?" Vikram demanded.

"Devki."

The name landed like a stone in water.

Devki Shah. Floor worker, ten years at Apex, assigned to various departments over time. The person their materials had identified as "The Gray Character"—an employee-level observer who spread cynicism and undermined positivity.

"Devki doesn't have technical knowledge to—" Dev started.

"Devki's been here ten years," Kavita interrupted. "Rotated through maintenance, operations, quality control. She's seen everything. Knows everyone. And she's been vocal about thinking leadership is incompetent and the plant deserves to fail."

Suresh nodded slowly. "I've heard her. Break room conversations. She's always the one saying 'they don't care about us' and 'this place is doomed' and 'leadership is just protecting themselves.'"

"That's not a crime," Priya said. "Being cynical doesn't make someone a saboteur."

"No, but it's motive," Vikram said. "If you genuinely believe the place is toxic and dying anyway, maybe you accelerate it. Mercy killing."

"Or proving a point," Ramesh added. "Showing that leadership really is dysfunctional by creating a situation where we'd turn on each other."

Meera pulled out her phone. "Security, can you tell me if Devki Shah was scheduled for any shift this weekend?"

She waited, listening.

"She wasn't scheduled, but... she has access credentials because she sometimes covers night shift maintenance. Check if her card was used... Saturday night, early Sunday morning."

Longer pause. Meera's expression changed.

"1:17 AM. East entrance. Thank you."

She put down the phone.

"It was Devki's credentials."

The room erupted.

"That doesn't mean she personally—"

"Who else would have her credentials?"

"This could be a setup—"

"We need to bring her in immediately—"

"Call the police—"

"STOP!" Meera's voice cut through the chaos. "Everyone stop talking."

Silence.

"Here's what we're not going to do: rush to conclusions. Here's what we are going to do: call the police, tell them we have a lead, let them handle the investigation properly. If Devki did this, they'll find evidence. If she didn't, we don't destroy someone's life based on access logs."

She pulled out her phone and made the call.

While she was talking to the police, Priya leaned over to Arvind.

"Do you believe it was her?" she asked quietly.

"I believe her credentials were used. Whether she used them, or someone used them to frame her, or she loaned them to someone else—I don't know yet."

"But you think there's more to this."

"I think it's almost too neat. Three days of investigation with no leads, and suddenly we find credentials usage that points to exactly the kind of person we'd want to blame—a cynical floor worker who's been vocal about leadership failures."

"You think it's a setup."

"I think we should be very careful about accepting easy answers when nothing else about this has been easy."

Within an hour, police had brought Devki in for questioning.

Within two hours, they'd searched her home and found the override mechanism in her garage, poorly hidden under a tarp.

Within three hours, she'd confessed.

Sort of.

"I took it," Devki said, sitting in the conference room with police officers flanking her. Meera and Arvind were allowed to observe. "I took the override. But I wasn't trying to blow anything up. I was trying to prove a point."

"What point?" the senior officer asked.

"That the safety systems here are garbage. That anyone with basic knowledge could compromise critical equipment. That leadership doesn't actually care about safety—they care about production numbers and looking good for corporate."

"So you risked killing people to prove a point about safety?"

"I didn't risk killing anyone! I know that reactor. I know the systems. I removed the override but I also adjusted the monitoring parameters to trigger alarms well before actual danger. The emergency happened exactly as I planned—loud, scary, but not actually dangerous. Not if the night crew did their jobs."

"Which they almost didn't," Arvind said quietly. "You gave them eight minutes to manually override a system they'd never had to manually override before. People could have died."

"But they didn't. Because I know this plant. I know what the backup systems can handle."

"Why?" Meera asked. "Why do this at all?"

Devki looked at her with something like pity.

"Because I'm tired. Tired of watching this place slowly die. Tired of watching you all fight each other while pretending it's leadership. Tired of showing up every day to a plant that's bleeding out while management holds team-building sessions and talks about 'alignment.'"

"So you decided to destroy what's left?"

"I decided to force honesty. You were all pretending Saturday's session fixed things. It didn't. You're still the same dysfunctional group, just temporarily playing nice. I proved it. Took one incident and you all turned on each other immediately."

"Because you gave us reason to."

"I gave you an excuse. The distrust was already there. I just exposed it."

Arvind studied her carefully. "You did this alone? No one helped you?"

A flicker of something crossed Devki's face. Hesitation.

"Alone," she said finally.

"You're sure? Because removing that override mechanism requires tools. Specific tools. And you'd need to know exactly how it was secured, which isn't common knowledge."

"I've worked maintenance. I know tools."

"And you knew exactly where to find the override, how to remove it, where to hide it, all without being clearly identified on camera?"

"I've been here ten years. I know this plant better than most of you."

"I believe you," Arvind said. "I just don't believe you acted alone."

The police officers exchanged glances.

"Do you have evidence of an accomplice?" one asked.

"Not yet. But I have questions about logistics that don't add up for a single person operation."

"I acted alone," Devki repeated, but her voice was less certain now.

They questioned her for another two hours. She stuck to her story. Acted alone. Wanted to prove a point. Never intended real harm.

The police arrested her. Criminal sabotage. Reckless endangerment. She'd face charges, trial, prison time.

Case closed, apparently.

But as Meera and Arvind walked back to the leadership conference room where everyone was waiting, Arvind said quietly:

"She's protecting someone."

"You think someone else was involved?"

"I think she's a true believer. She genuinely believes leadership is corrupt and the plant is doomed. But someone gave her the idea. Someone with more strategic thinking than an angry floor worker. Someone who knew that Saturday's session made us vulnerable to exactly this kind of division."

"Who?"

"I don't know. But we should find out before we congratulate ourselves on solving this."

They entered the conference room. Everyone looked up expectantly.

"It was Devki," Meera announced. "She confessed. She's been arrested."

Relief flooded the room. Not happiness—the situation was still terrible—but relief that at least they knew. At least it wasn't one of them. At least the paranoia could end.

"So we can restart operations?" Vikram asked.

"As of now, yes. Full restart tomorrow morning."

"And corporate?"

"Still want us at the board meeting Thursday. But at least we can tell them we identified the saboteur and resolved the situation."

"One disturbed employee," Rajesh said. "That's the narrative. Not systemic dysfunction. Just one bad actor."

"Is that what we believe?" Kavita asked quietly.

"Does it matter?" Vikram responded. "It's what we're telling corporate."

Priya stood up. "It matters because if Devki was right—if we're still the same dysfunctional team just pretending otherwise—then solving the sabotage doesn't solve anything. We're still failing. Just slower."

"What do you want from us, Priya?" Vikram's voice was tired. "We tried your unity session. It lasted two days before someone literally sabotaged us. Maybe dysfunction isn't fixable. Maybe we just manage it as best we can until corporate shuts us down."

"Is that really what you believe?"

Vikram looked at her for a long moment. "I believe we're nine people trying to save a sinking ship with a bucket. And no amount of team-building changes that math."

The meeting ended without resolution. People dispersed, exhausted, relieved, still uncertain.

Only Arvind stayed behind, writing in his notebook.

Meera sat down next to him. "What are you writing?"

"Questions that don't have answers yet."

"Like?"

"Like why Devki seemed almost relieved when she confessed. Like why she was so specific about acting alone when no one had accused her of having help. Like why someone who's been here ten years and knows these systems intimately would choose a method that was theatrical but not actually effective."

"You think she's covering for someone."

"I think she's the visible part of something larger. And I think we're about to declare victory while the real problem goes unidentified."

"Even if you're right, what can we do? The police investigated. She confessed. We don't have evidence of anything else."

"No. But we have patterns. And patterns tell stories if you know how to read them."

He closed his notebook and stood up.

"Get some rest, Meera. Thursday's going to be brutal regardless."

After he left, Meera sat alone in the empty conference room, looking at the whiteboard that still had their Saturday commitments written on it.

I commit to trusting people to handle things.

I commit to making decisions with imperfect information.

I commit to balancing empathy with accountability.

I commit to being less of a tyrant.

I commit to listening to concerns.

I commit to being direct instead of political.

I commit to using humor to build us up.

I commit to asking for help before I break.

I commit to holding us accountable.

Three days ago, those commitments had felt meaningful.

Now they felt like artifacts from another world. A world before they learned how fragile unity really was.

Meera erased the board slowly, watching the words disappear under the felt eraser.

Maybe Vikram was right. Maybe dysfunction wasn't fixable.

Maybe the best they could hope for was to manage the decline with whatever dignity they had left.

She turned off the lights and locked the door behind her, carrying that thought into a dark Tuesday evening.

Tomorrow, they'd restart the plant.

Thursday, they'd face corporate.

And somewhere in between, they'd have to decide: were they nine leaders trying to save something worth saving?

Or just nine people managing the inevitable end?

The answer, she suspected, would determine everything.

12

THE LAST SHIFT

The corporate presentation was scheduled for 10:00 AM Thursday at the Ahmedabad headquarters. Travel time: ninety minutes. Which meant leaving Nadiad by 8:00 AM at the latest.

Meera woke up at 4:30 AM and knew immediately she wouldn't be going back to sleep.

Her presentation was ready. Forty-three slides documenting the sabotage incident, their response, the investigation, the resolution. Eighteen more slides about operational recovery plans, financial projections, and the path forward.

Together, they looked out at a new horizon.

It was a good presentation. Professional. Thorough. Complete.

It was also, she knew in her gut, not going to be enough.

Corporate wasn't just evaluating their response to the sabotage. They were evaluating whether Apex Chemicals Nadiad was worth keeping alive.

And the answer, based on six months of declining numbers and increasing dysfunction, was probably no.

She made coffee. Stared at her laptop. Added three more slides, then deleted them. Reworded a conclusion, then changed it back.

At 6:00 AM, her phone buzzed. A message from Priya:

Can we meet before we leave? My office. 7:00.

Meera typed back: I'll be there.

At 7:00 AM exactly, she walked into Priya's office to find not just Priya, but all of them. Arvind, Kavita, Vikram, Dev, Rajesh, Ramesh, Suresh. Even the lead engineer Prakash Reddy.

"What's this?" Meera asked.

"Insurance," Priya said. "Sit down."

Meera sat.

"We've been up all night," Priya continued. "Working on something. Because your presentation—the one corporate asked for—it's fine. It checks the boxes. But it doesn't save us."

"I'm open to suggestions, but we leave in an hour—"

"We're not suggesting changes to your presentation," Arvind interrupted. "We're suggesting a completely different approach."

He pulled out his laptop, connected it to Priya's monitor, and pulled up a presentation Meera had never seen before.

The title slide read:

APEX CHEMICALS NADIAD: THE REAL STORY YOU NEED TO HEAR

"What is this?" Meera asked.

"The truth," Kavita said quietly. "Not the corporate-friendly version. The actual truth about what's happening here, why it's happening, and what it would take to fix it."

"Corporate doesn't want truth. They want reassurance that we can recover."

"They want justification for a decision they've already made," Vikram said. "We've all seen it before. The numbers have been declining for months. The sabotage was just the excuse they needed. They're shutting us down. Your presentation just makes it easier for them to feel good about it."

"So what are you proposing?"

Dev leaned forward. "We stop playing defense. We go on offense. We tell them exactly how they created this situation, exactly what it would take to actually fix it, and exactly what happens if they shut us down."

"That's… that's career suicide."

"Maybe," Rajesh admitted. "Or maybe it's the only thing that forces an actual conversation instead of a predetermined conclusion."

Meera looked around the room. Nine people who'd spent months fighting each other, who'd suspected each other of sabotage days ago, who'd barely survived their dysfunction.

And now they were united. Finally. At the worst possible moment.

"Walk me through it," she said.

Arvind advanced to the first slide.

SLIDE 2: What Corporate Thinks Is Happening

- Production decline due to poor management
- Sabotage due to employee dissatisfaction
- Leadership dysfunction preventing recovery
- Facility is terminal; relocate operations

"This is their narrative," Arvind said. "It's neat. It's clean. It puts blame at the facility level and keeps corporate blameless. And it's about forty percent true."

SLIDE 3: What's Actually Happening

• Systematic underinvestment in equipment maintenance

• Impossible targets with declining resources

• Corporate pressure prioritizing short-term numbers over long-term sustainability

• Leadership team responding to contradictory demands with predictable dysfunction

Kavita spoke up. "We've been blaming each other for things that are symptoms of systemic problems. Yes, we're dysfunctional. But we're dysfunctional because we've been set up to fail."

SLIDE 4: The Real Numbers

Rajesh had built this one. Financial data showing:

• Equipment maintenance budget cut 37% over three years

• Staffing reduced 23% while production targets increased 18%

• Training budget eliminated entirely

• Quality control resources cut in half

"You can't cut investment, increase demands, and expect better results," Rajesh said. "That's not management. That's magical thinking."

SLIDE 5: The Human Cost

Suresh had contributed to this one. Data on:

• Employee turnover increased 340% in eighteen months

• Stress-related medical claims up 290%

• Safety incidents increased 180%

• Three documented mental health crises—including his own, which he'd disclosed for this presentation

"We're not just failing mechanically," Suresh said, voice quiet but steady. "We're failing people. Including ourselves."

SLIDE 6: The Leadership Response

Priya's section. Honest documentation of their dysfunction:

• Nine different leadership approaches with no coordination

• Meetings that produced arguments instead of decisions

• Personal conflicts prioritized over organizational needs

• An attempted sabotage that exposed how little trust existed

"We're not pretending we were functional," Priya said. "We weren't. But we're owning it. And more importantly, we're showing how we changed."

The next section documented their Saturday session. The commitments they'd made. The framework they'd built. And then:

SLIDE 11: What We've Accomplished In Three Days

Despite the sabotage, despite the shutdown, they'd done something remarkable:

• Established daily coordination meetings (actually happening, with documented outcomes)

• Cross-department shadowing started (Vikram spent four hours in Kavita's world yesterday, came back different)

• Decision framework implemented (tested three times already, working)

• Automation pilot approved (small scale, Reactor 6, starting next week)

• Performance standards redefined (Vikram and Kavita built it together)

• Support systems for struggling employees established (Suresh had help now, real help)

"Three days," Ramesh said. "We turned this ship in three days once we stopped fighting each other and started fighting the actual problems."

SLIDE 15: What We Need From Corporate

Dev's section. Specific, costed, realistic:

• ₹85 lakhs for critical equipment upgrades (not nice-to-have; must-have)

• 12% staff increase to match production demands realistically

• Six-month reduction in production targets while systems stabilize

• Autonomy to run the facility without weekly interference

• Commitment to three-year evaluation timeline instead of quarterly panic

"This isn't a bailout," Dev said. "It's an actual investment in an actual turnaround. Everything here pays for itself within eighteen months if you give us room to implement it."

SLIDE 18: What Happens If You Shut Us Down

Vikram's section. Brutal, honest:

• 847 direct job losses in a city where Apex is the major employer

• Supply chain disruption affecting 34 companies

• Loss of specialized pharmaceutical compound production capability that takes years to rebuild elsewhere

• Immediate client defection to international competitors

• Regional economic impact estimated at ₹340 crores over five years

• And most importantly: Corporate would be killing a facility that's demonstrably salvageable

"You can shut us down," Vikram said. "You have that authority. But you'd be making the wrong call based on incomplete information during the exact moment we figured out how to fix this."

The final section was Meera's:

SLIDE 25: What We're Asking For

One word: Trust.

Trust that we've learned from our failures. Trust that we can execute what we're proposing. Trust that three days of actual unity is the beginning of sustainable change, not a temporary anomaly. Trust that we're worth the investment.

And if we're wrong—if we fail again despite this support—then shut us down with clear conscience.

But give us the chance to prove we're not failing anymore.

Arvind closed the presentation.

"That's what we have," he said. "Forty-eight hours of work. Nine people who finally agreed on something. The truth, the plan, and a request for actual support instead of managed decline."

Meera sat back, overwhelmed.

"This is… this is not what corporate expects."

"No," Priya agreed. "But it's what they need to hear."

"It could backfire completely. They could see this as insubordination. As blaming them for our failures."

"It could," Rajesh admitted. "Or it could be the first honest conversation they've had with a facility in years. Corporate lives in spreadsheets and reports. We're showing them reality. There's risk in that. But there's also opportunity."

Meera looked at each of them. Really looked at them.

Three days ago, they'd been ready to destroy each other over suspicion of sabotage.

Now they were unified, strategic, willing to risk everything on a truth-telling mission that could end their careers.

"If we do this," Meera said slowly, "we go all in. No hedging. No backing down if they push back. We present this exactly as you built it, and we stand behind it."

Nine heads nodded.

"Okay," Meera said. "Let's go save this thing."

The drive to Ahmedabad was quiet. They took two cars—Meera, Priya, Arvind, and Kavita in one; Vikram, Dev, Rajesh, Ramesh, and Suresh in the other.

In the first car, Kavita broke the silence: "Are we insane?"

"Probably," Arvind said.

"But we're insane together," Priya added. "That's different."

"Is it?" Kavita asked.

"We're about to find out."

At 9:45 AM, they walked into Apex Chemicals corporate headquarters—a glass and steel building that smelled like air conditioning and ambition. Everything here was clean, climate-controlled, far removed from the chemical smell and heat of actual manufacturing.

The corporate team was already assembled in the main conference room. Six executives, three board members, two consultants who were clearly there to recommend closure and asset liquidation.

The CEO—Harish Kapoor, early sixties, made his career in finance, never worked a plant floor in his life—sat at the head of the table.

"Meera. Team. Please, sit."

They sat. Nine of them on one side of the table. Eleven corporate representatives on the other.

Harish glanced at his watch. "We have ninety minutes. Let's begin. Meera, I understand you have a presentation on the sabotage incident and recovery plan?"

"I do," Meera said. "But if you'll permit, we'd like to present something else first."

Harish frowned. "We asked for a specific—"

"I know what you asked for. And we can provide that. But I think you need to hear something else first. It'll take thirty minutes. If after that you want the original presentation, we'll provide it. But please—thirty minutes."

Harish exchanged glances with the other executives. Finally: "Proceed."

For the next thirty minutes, they walked through it. Every slide. Every data point. Every honest admission of their failures and every clear demand for what they needed.

The room was silent except for their voices.

Meera watched the corporate team's faces. Some looked uncomfortable. Some looked defensive. The consultants looked offended—this wasn't how failing facilities were supposed to behave. You were supposed to accept blame gracefully, not redirect it upward.

When they finished, silence.

Finally, Harish spoke. "That was… certainly direct."

"It was honest," Meera said.

"It was accusatory," one of the board members said. "You're essentially blaming corporate for your facility's failures."

"We're identifying systemic issues that contributed to those failures," Arvind corrected. "Including our own dysfunction. We're not claiming innocence. We're claiming the full picture is more complex than 'bad facility management.'"

"The bottom line," one of the consultants said, "is that your facility is losing money. Has been for months. The sabotage incident was simply the final indicator that operations there are untenable."

"The sabotage incident was one person's misguided attempt to prove a point," Kavita said. "It wasn't representative of systemic employee dissatisfaction. It was an individual act that we investigated, resolved, and learned from."

"And your leadership team?" another executive asked. "The reports we've been receiving suggest significant dysfunction at the management level."

"There was," Priya admitted. "Past tense. Three days ago, we were nine separate agendas. Today, we're unified behind a common plan. That transformation matters."

"Transformation that took how long? Months of deteriorating performance?"

"Transformation that took finally being honest with each other," Vikram said. "Which nobody encouraged us to do. Including corporate. You wanted positive reports and recovery promises. We gave you those. They were lies. This"—he gestured at their presentation—"this is the truth. We were failing. We know why. We know how to fix it. The question is whether you'll give us the resources to do so."

"The investment you're requesting—" an executive pulled up numbers on their tablet—"eighty-five lakhs in equipment, staff increases, target reductions. That's substantial."

"That's necessary," Dev said. "Every item on that list pays for itself in measurable ways within eighteen months. We're not asking for charity. We're asking for rational investment in a salvageable facility."

Harish leaned back. "And if we don't provide this investment? What then?"

"Then you shut us down," Meera said simply. "That's your prerogative. But you'll be shutting down a facility that was broken by underinvestment and is now ready to recover with proper support. You'll be proving that corporate doesn't actually support turnarounds—they support managed decline until closure becomes inevitable."

"That's not fair—"

"It's accurate," Arvind interrupted. "And more importantly, it's observable. Show me a struggling Apex facility in the last five years that received increased investment and autonomy. I can show you three that received budget cuts and increased oversight until they collapsed. That's a pattern. Patterns reveal strategy."

The room went tense.

One of the board members spoke up—an older woman named Geeta Patel who'd been quiet until now. "You make compelling points. But you're asking us to bet on nine leaders who, by your own admission, were dysfunctional until a few days ago. Why should we believe this unity is sustainable?"

"Because dysfunction was rational given the conditions we were operating under," Priya said. "Contradictory demands, insufficient resources, constant pressure with no support. We responded by fragmenting, by protecting our own departments, by fighting each other for scraps. That made sense in that environment. But the environment changed. We changed it. Saturday's session, the sabotage response, the last three days—we built new patterns. And new patterns, if reinforced, become new culture."

"That's very theoretical."

"It's behavioral science. Which is more reliable than hoping people magically improve without changing circumstances."

Geeta Patel smiled slightly. "You've clearly thought this through."

"We've had no choice," Suresh said quietly. It was the first time he'd spoken in the meeting. "When you're drowning, you either figure out how to swim or you die. We figured out how to swim. Now we need you to throw us a rope instead of telling us the water's not that deep."

Silence.

Harish looked at his team, then back at the Nadiad leadership group.

"We need to discuss this internally. Can you wait outside?"

"Of course."

They filed out to a waiting area. Sat in uncomfortable corporate chairs. Didn't speak.

Twenty minutes passed. Thirty. Forty-five.

At the hour mark, Ramesh said quietly: "We're either getting dramatically fired or dramatically saved. There's no middle ground with a wait this long."

"Optimistic," Vikram muttered.

"I'm good at reading rooms. Some of them want to shut us down and be done with it. But Geeta Patel—she was listening. Really listening."

At seventy-three minutes, the door opened. Harish gestured them back in.

They sat. Waited.

Harish looked at each of them before speaking.

"We've reviewed your proposal. It's... unconventional. And

frank to the point of being uncomfortable. But it's also the most honest assessment we've received from any facility in years."

Pause.

"Here's our decision: We're giving you six months. Full six months. During that time, you'll receive the eighty-five lakhs for equipment upgrades, authorization for a ten percent staff increase, and a twenty percent reduction in production targets for the first quarter."

Relief began to surface—but Harish held up a hand.

"Conditions: You implement everything you proposed. The coordination meetings. The decision framework. The cross-department collaboration. The pilot automation program. All of it. And you report to me directly—weekly updates, no filters, same honesty you showed today. If in six months you're meeting adjusted targets, showing improved efficiency, and demonstrating sustainable leadership function, we continue investment. If you're not—we shut down Nadiad and consolidate operations in Bangalore. Clear?"

"Clear," Meera said.

"One more thing." Harish looked directly at their group. "We're assigning a leadership consultant to work with you. Not to take over. To observe, support, and help sustain the transformation you claim you've started. You'll meet with them weekly. Non-negotiable."

"Agreed," Meera said.

"Then congratulations. You just bought yourselves six months and about a thousand second chances. Don't waste them."

The drive back to Nadiad was different. Lighter. Not celebratory—they all knew how much work was ahead—but genuinely hopeful.

"We did it," Kavita said, almost disbelieving.

"We did something," Arvind corrected. "Whether we actually succeed depends on the next six months."

"Always the optimist," Vikram said, but there was no edge in it.

When they arrived back at the plant, word had already spread. The full workforce was gathered in the main courtyard—operators, technicians, supervisors, support staff. Eight hundred forty-seven people waiting to hear whether they still had jobs.

Meera stood on the platform used for safety announcements and looked out at the crowd. These were faces she recognized now—not just from org charts and shift rosters, but from floor walks and tea stall conversations and the slow, painful work of actually learning who people were.

"We went to corporate today expecting to defend our continued existence," she said, voice carrying across the crowd. "Instead, we told them the truth. About what's been happening here. About what we need to fix it. About what we're capable of if given the chance."

Pause.

"They gave us six months. Full support. Real investment. The opportunity to prove that this facility is worth saving."

The response was immediate—not wild celebration, but the sound of eight hundred people exhaling at once. Relief. The possibility of a future.

"But I need to be clear about something," Meera continued. "This only works if all of us—leadership and floor workers—actually change. The dysfunction wasn't just at the management level. It's been everywhere. The cynicism. The finger-pointing. The giving up. That stops now."

She paused, finding words for what came next carefully.

"It also requires honesty about what happened. About Devki. About the sabotage. She made a terrible choice. But she made it because she believed—correctly—that things were broken. We're not excusing what she did. But we're acknowledging why she believed it needed to be done. And we're committing to building a place where that kind of desperation doesn't make sense anymore."

The crowd was quiet now, listening.

"Six months. We have six months to transform this facility from failing to functional. Leadership's committed. Are you?"

People responded—not polished applause, but something rawer. Real. Someone near the back shouted "Finally!" and a ripple of laughter moved through the crowd, warm and exhausted and human.

As people dispersed and returned to work, the leadership team stood together in the emptying courtyard. Nobody said anything for a moment. They'd spent months being nine separate disasters. Right now, in the cooling afternoon air, they were just nine tired people who'd somehow pulled it off.

Ramesh broke the silence. "Solid 8 out of 10. Would've been higher if Meera had done a mic drop."

"I don't have a mic," Meera said.

"Metaphorical mic drop. Learn your leadership theater."

People laughed. Real laughs.

"First coordination meeting is tomorrow, 8:00 AM," Priya said, pulling out her phone. "Everyone clear?"

Nods around the group.

"Good. Get some rest. Tomorrow we start actually doing the work."

As people dispersed, Meera found herself standing with Arvind at the edge of the courtyard. The plant hummed behind them, second shift beginning its routines.

"Do you think we can actually do this?" she asked.

Arvind considered the question in his careful way. "I think we have a sixty-two percent chance of success based on historical data about organizational turnarounds."

"That's not very reassuring."

"It wasn't meant to be reassuring. It was meant to be honest." He paused. "But I also think we have something most turnarounds don't have."

"Which is?"

"Nine leaders who finally understand that being right individually matters less than being effective collectively. That's not nothing."

"Is it enough?"

Arvind looked back at the plant—at the reactors they'd nearly lost, the workers filing through the gates, the building that still stood after everything.

"We're about to find out," he said.

He walked toward his car, notebook tucked under his arm.

Meera stood there a moment longer, alone in the courtyard, feeling the full weight of the day settle into something she didn't have a precise word for.

Not triumph. Not relief. Something quieter than both.

She'd made decisions today with imperfect information, in front of people who could have ended her career. She'd trusted nine difficult, flawed, remarkable people to stand with her. And they had.

Tomorrow the work would continue—harder, slower, less dramatic than today. Targets to meet. Systems to fix. Trust to rebuild one small interaction at a time.

But tonight, Apex Chemicals still stood.

Eight hundred forty-seven families would eat because of what happened in this building.

And that, for now, was enough.

EPILOGUE: THE NEW FOUNDATION

Six Months Later

The numbers were posted in the main break room where everyone could see them:

Q3 PERFORMANCE METRICS:

• Production efficiency: 87% (target: 85%)

• Quality rating: 94% (target: 90%)

• Safety incidents: 2 (industry average: 7)

• Employee satisfaction: 78% (previous: 41%)

• Client retention: 96%

• New client acquisitions: 3

Not perfect. But alive. More than alive—thriving in a way that felt fragile still, but real.

Meera stood looking at the board, coffee in hand, watching the morning shift change. 6:00 AM, the time when the plant transitioned from night to day, when workers clustered near the tea stall outside Gate 2 for those precious few minutes of being human before becoming operators and technicians again.

Except now, supervisors were out there too. Including Vikram, of all people, who was actually listening to someone's story about their daughter's school admission instead of barking orders.

Small things. Everything was small things now.

The equipment upgrades were complete—Reactor 3 running better than it had in five years, Reactor 6 fully automated and exceeding projections. The new hires had integrated smoothly, bringing fresh energy without the cynicism that had poisoned the culture before. The weekly leadership coordination meetings that Meera had dreaded initially had become... not easy, but functional. Sometimes even productive.

They still argued. God, did they argue.

Last week, Dev and Arvind had spent forty-five minutes debating the risk parameters for the Reactor 4 expansion. Vikram had called Kavita "impossibly idealistic" during a performance review discussion. Rajesh had tried to negotiate better supplier terms without telling Suresh first, which led to a tense hour of untangling communication failures.

But the difference was: they worked through it.

They didn't fracture. Didn't retreat to their corners. Didn't let disagreement become personal warfare.

They'd learned—slowly, painfully—that conflict was okay. Necessary, even. What wasn't okay was the avoidance, the politics, the pretending they agreed when they didn't.

"Morning, Meera."

Priya appeared beside her, also holding coffee, also watching the floor come alive.

"Morning. You're here early."

"Couldn't sleep. Brain wouldn't shut off."

"Good brain thoughts or bad brain thoughts?"

"Cautiously optimistic brain thoughts. Which feels weird. I'm not used to optimism that isn't immediately followed by disaster."

Meera laughed. "Same. I keep waiting for the other shoe to drop."

"Maybe there is no other shoe. Maybe we actually fixed this thing."

"Or maybe we're in the eye of the storm and just don't know it yet."

They stood in comfortable silence for a moment, watching their plant—their saved plant—operate smoothly.

Kavita arrived at 6:15, like always, making her rounds, stopping to talk to operators, asking about families and health and life outside these walls. But now she also asked about performance metrics, about process improvements, about quality concerns. Empathy and accountability, living together. Who knew that was possible?

Arvind was already at his observation deck post, notebook out, but today he was writing recommendations instead of just observations. Two days ago, he'd made a decision about a supplier change with only seventy percent certainty instead of his usual ninety-five percent. The decision had been correct. He'd been quietly pleased about it for days.

Dev was in the automation control room, training two operators on the new systems. Teaching instead of preaching. Listening instead of dismissing. His proposals still came regularly—he couldn't help himself—but now they were collaborative documents instead of manifestos. Amazing what happened when you treated people like partners instead of obstacles.

Suresh walked in at 6:45, no longer the first one here and no longer staying until midnight. Regular hours. Delegated responsibilities. A procurement team that actually functioned instead of one stressed manager drowning alone. He'd even taken a vacation last month—a real one, phone turned off, no emails. Came back human.

Rajesh still worked his networks, still built relationships, still operated in that gray space between strategy and politics. But he'd gotten more transparent about it. Last week, he'd forwarded an email to the full leadership team showing a supplier trying to bribe him for preferential treatment. Old Rajesh would have handled it quietly, maybe even leveraged it. New Rajesh made it a teaching moment about ethics and transparency.

Ramesh wandered in at 7:00, immediately gravitating toward a cluster of workers who were laughing about something. He joined in, added his own joke, and the laughter grew. But then—and this was the change—he transitioned the conversation to something real. Someone's upcoming surgery. Someone else's kid's college admission. Real care, not just deflection. Humor as connection instead of armor.

Vikram arrived at 7:30, which was late for him. But he'd been at his daughter's school function the night before—actually attended, stayed for the whole thing, turned his phone off. She'd been shocked. He'd been present. The work had survived without him for three hours.

He still pushed hard. Still had high standards. Still occasionally crossed the line into harshness. But when Kavita called him on it —which she did now, regularly—he listened. Adjusted. Apologized, even, which six months ago would have been unthinkable.

At 8:00 AM, they gathered for their weekly coordination meeting. Same conference room where they'd spent months destroying each other. Different energy entirely now.

"Okay," Meera started, pulling up the week's agenda. "Three items: Q3 review debrief, Reactor 7 maintenance schedule, and the new client proposal from BioGenix."

They worked through it systematically. Arvind provided data analysis. Vikram raised operational concerns. Kavita flagged worker impact issues. Dev suggested technical improvements. Rajesh outlined supplier implications. Suresh confirmed procurement capacity. Ramesh kept them human when the discussion got too abstract. Priya facilitated when tensions rose.

Not perfect. But functional.

They made decisions. Real decisions. Sometimes unanimous, sometimes by majority, sometimes by deferring to whoever had the most expertise in that specific area.

The decision framework they'd built six months ago—the thing that seemed so theoretical during that Saturday session—had become muscle memory.

By 9:00 AM, they were done. Decisions made. Actions assigned. Next week's agenda set.

As people filed out, Anjali—the leadership consultant corporate had assigned—caught Meera's attention.

"Can we talk?"

They sat. Anjali pulled out her tablet, scrolling through notes.

"I'm wrapping up my assessment," she said. "Corporate asked for a final evaluation of whether the turnaround is sustainable or if you just had a good quarter."

Meera's stomach tightened. "And?"

"And I'm recommending they extend investment for another eighteen months and reduce oversight. You don't need a consultant anymore. You need to be left alone to run your facility."

Relief flooded through Meera. "You're sure?"

"I've been doing this for twelve years. I've seen facilities fake functionality until consultants leave. This isn't that. You've internalized the changes. The conflicts you have now are productive conflicts. The decisions you make are informed by multiple perspectives. The culture shift is real."

She paused.

"I'm not saying you're perfect. Dev still pushes too hard sometimes. Vikram still has an edge. Suresh still struggles with stress. But you're managing it. You're aware of your patterns and actively working to improve them. That's all anyone can ask."

"What convinced you?" Meera asked. "That it was real?"

Anjali smiled. "Last week. The argument about the maintenance schedule. Vikram wanted to defer it to hit production targets. Kavita pushed back about worker safety. It got heated. And then Vikram stopped mid-argument and said 'You're right. I'm prioritizing numbers over people again. We do the maintenance.' Just like that. Changed his position because someone made a good point. That's not performance. That's actual growth."

After Anjali left, Meera sat alone in the empty conference room.

Six months ago, this room had been a war zone. Nine people fighting for survival in nine different directions.

Now it was just a room where work got done.

Not dramatic. Not inspiring. Just... functional.

And functional, it turned out, was everything.

At noon, Meera did something she hadn't done in months: she left for lunch. Actually left. Drove to a small restaurant in town, sat down, ate slowly, didn't check her phone obsessively.

When she returned at 1:15, the plant was still standing. Shocking.

She found Priya in her office, working on next month's staffing plans.

"I just had lunch," Meera announced.

Priya looked up. "Congratulations?"

"No, I mean I left the building. For a full hour. And nothing exploded."

"Welcome to delegation. It's nice here."

Meera sat down. "Do you think we actually did it? Not just survived, but actually transformed this place?"

Priya considered the question carefully. "I think we transformed ourselves. The place followed. Whether it's permanent or temporary—I don't know. But right now, in this moment? Yes. We did it."

"It's weird, right? Six months ago, we were dying. Now we're..."

"Functional?"

"I was going to say 'boring.' In a good way. Like, we're just a normal chemical plant doing normal plant things. No drama. No crisis. Just work."

"That's success," Priya said. "Success is boring. It's showing up every day, making incremental improvements, solving small problems before they become big ones. It's not cinematic. But it works."

A knock on the door. Arvind poked his head in.

"Sorry to interrupt. Meera, corporate just sent the Q4 projections. They're increasing our targets."

Meera's first instinct was panic. More targets meant more pressure meant more chances to fail meant—

She stopped herself.

"By how much?"

"Twelve percent."

"Can we handle it?"

Arvind pulled out his notebook. "With the new automation and current staffing? Yes. Seventy-eight percent probability of success. Which, for me, counts as high confidence."

"Okay. Let's build a plan. Get Dev and Suresh involved. We'll present it at Monday's meeting."

Arvind nodded and left.

Meera looked at Priya. "Did I just handle that calmly?"

"You did. Character growth. It's very touching."

They both laughed.

At 5:00 PM, as the day shift ended, Meera did one final walk of the floor.

She found Sunita at Reactor 4, training a new employee—a young guy named Ravi who looked barely old enough to drink, let alone operate complex chemical equipment.

"How's he doing?" Meera asked.

"Good. Fast learner. Asks good questions."

Ravi looked nervous being addressed by the Operations Director. "I'm trying, ma'am. There's a lot to learn."

"That's the job. Lot to learn, lot of responsibility. But you've got good people teaching you."

She moved on, letting Sunita continue the training.

Near Reactor 6—their automation pilot, now their showcase success—she found Dev explaining something to a group of operators who'd initially resisted the automated systems.

"—and that's why the sensor redundancy matters. You're not being replaced. You're being equipped with better tools. Your judgment still matters. Your experience still matters. The technology just removes the tedious parts."

One of the operators asked a question about override protocols. Dev answered patiently, thoroughly, without a trace of condescension.

Who was this person, and what had he done with the missionary zealot from six months ago?

At Reactor 3—their crisis point, their near-catastrophe, now running better than ever—Prakash Reddy was doing routine checks.

"How's she running?" Meera asked.

"Beautifully. Honestly, better than in years. The upgrades made a real difference."

"Think she's good for another decade?"

"At least. Maybe more if we keep up proper maintenance."

Proper maintenance. Funded maintenance. The crazy idea that investing in equipment prevented disasters.

Revolutionary stuff.

She finished her walk and headed to her office to pack up for the day. On her desk was a handwritten note:

Boss—

Three of us from the floor wanted you to know: it's different here now. Better. We actually want to come to work again. Don't know what changed with you all, but whatever it is, keep doing it.

— The Night Shift

Meera folded the note carefully and put it in her desk drawer, next to the others that had been appearing over the past few months.

Evidence. Proof that the changes weren't just in their heads. That something real had shifted.

She turned off her computer, turned off her office lights, and walked out to the parking lot.

The sun was setting over the reactor halls, painting everything in orange and gold. The plant looked almost beautiful like this. Almost peaceful.

Her phone buzzed. A message in the leadership group chat that Priya had created:

Priya: *Pizza at my place Saturday. 7 PM. Spouses/partners invited. This is not a work meeting. This is humans eating food together.*

Ramesh: *Does pineapple belong on pizza? Discuss.*

Vikram: *If you put pineapple on pizza at this gathering, I'm leaving.*

Kavita: *Vikram, you have opinions about pizza toppings but not about worker dignity? Interesting priorities.*

Vikram: *I have evolved. But I haven't evolved enough to accept fruit on pizza.*

Dev: *Technically, tomatoes are fruit, so...*

Arvind: *This conversation has a 94% probability of devolving into chaos.*

Rajesh: *I'll bring wine. Good wine, not the cheap stuff.*

Suresh: *I'll bring dessert. My wife makes excellent gulab jamun.*

Meera: *I'll be there. No pineapple pizza. I value harmony.*

Priya: *You're all impossible and I love it.*

Meera smiled, put her phone away, and drove home through evening traffic that felt less suffocating than it used to.

Six months ago, she'd been driving this same route wondering if she'd have a job in a week.

Now she was driving home from work that felt like work—challenging, sometimes frustrating, occasionally overwhelming, but manageable.

Normal.

Functional.

Boring in the best possible way.

The plant would still be there tomorrow. The problems would still exist—equipment would break, targets would challenge them, people would occasionally drive her crazy.

But they'd handle it. Together. As a team that was flawed but functional, imperfect but improving, human but trying.

And somewhere in that trying, they'd found something that almost looked like hope.

No, not hope.

Something better.

Certainty that whatever came next, they could face it.

Not because they were perfect.

But because they'd learned—finally—how to be imperfect together.

And that, it turned out, was enough.

There was one more thing that happened in those six months that didn't appear on any performance metric board.

Devki Shah's case went to trial four months after her arrest. Criminal sabotage, reckless endangerment — the charges carried serious weight. Her defense argued intent: she never meant to cause actual harm, only to expose systemic failure. The prosecution argued that good intentions didn't make dangerous actions safe.

The court sentenced her to eighteen months, suspended on the condition of community service, a substantial fine, and mandatory counseling. No prison time, ultimately. The judge noted in his ruling that while her method was unacceptable and dangerous, the conditions she was responding to were real and documented.

Arvind's suspicion that she hadn't acted alone was never officially confirmed. The police investigation found no concrete evidence of an accomplice. Whether someone had planted the idea in her mind, encouraged her cynicism into action, or whether she had arrived at her terrible plan entirely alone — that question was quietly closed without a definitive answer. Some things, Arvind wrote in his notebook, resist resolution no matter how carefully you document them.

What Apex did in response mattered more than the verdict.

They created a formal worker feedback channel — anonymous, reviewed monthly by the full leadership team, with documented responses to every concern raised. They called it the Open Valve program. The name was Ramesh's idea, and for once nobody laughed at it.

Devki never returned to Apex. But three workers who had been closest to her — people who had shared her cynicism, her belief that nothing would ever change — did stay. And six months later, two of them had been promoted to senior operator positions.

Meera didn't know if that was justice. She wasn't sure justice was the right word for any of it.

But it felt like something. Like the plant had looked honestly at the worst version of itself and decided to become something different.

That, perhaps, was the only real conclusion the story could offer.

Three months after that...

Ravi Thakkar stood in the break room on his lunch break, looking at the updated numbers:

Q4 PERFORMANCE METRICS:

• Production efficiency: 91%

• Quality rating: 96%

• Safety incidents: 1

• Employee satisfaction: 82%

• Client retention: 98%

• New client acquisitions: 5

He'd been at Apex for three months now. Long enough to hear the stories about "before"—the chaos, the dysfunction, the near-collapse.

Hard to imagine, looking at the place now. Everything ran smoothly. Leadership was visible, accessible, seemed to actually care. People complained sometimes—about targets, about policies, about normal work stuff—but not about the fundamental dysfunction that the old-timers remembered.

Sunita sat down across from him with her lunch.

"You settling in okay?"

"Yeah. I like it here. Feels like a good place to build a career."

"It is now. Wasn't always."

"What changed?"

Sunita thought about it. "Leadership figured out how to lead, I guess. Stopped fighting each other. Started fighting for us."

"Think it'll last?"

"Who knows? Nothing lasts forever. But right now, today? Yeah. It's good."

Ravi nodded, filing that away.

He had ambitions. Wanted to move up, maybe become a supervisor someday, then a manager, eventually make a real impact.

He wondered what kind of leader he'd be. Would he be like Meera—steady, decisive, carrying the weight quietly? Like Vikram—demanding but fair, pushing people to be better? Like Kavita—caring, human, never forgetting the person behind the position?

Like Dev, challenging everything? Like Arvind, analyzing everything? Like any of them?

Probably he'd be himself. Whoever that turned out to be.

And maybe—if he was lucky, if he learned, if he paid attention—he'd figure out how to be himself in a way that helped instead of hurt. That built instead of destroyed. That acknowledged his flaws instead of weaponizing them.

Maybe.

He finished his lunch and headed back to Reactor 4, where Sunita was waiting to teach him advanced pressure management protocols.

The plant hummed around him. Machines running. People working. Life happening.

Eight hundred forty-seven families eating because of what happened in this building.

And nine leaders who'd learned—painfully, slowly, imperfectly—what it truly cost to lead.

Every flaw had a role.

Every role had a cost.

Every cost, it turned out, was worth paying.

If you knew what you were fighting for.

APPENDICES

APPENDIX A: LEADERSHIP REFLECTION GUIDE

Questions for readers to assess their own leadership style, strengths, and blind spots

Part 1: Identifying Your Primary Leadership Archetype

Read through each archetype description. Rate yourself on a scale of 1-5 (1 = not at all like me, 5 = very much like me) on how much you identify with each style.

The Calm Strategist (Arvind)

• I prefer to analyze situations thoroughly before making decisions

• People describe me as patient and observant

• I'm uncomfortable making decisions with incomplete information

• I document patterns and keep detailed records

• My strength is seeing the big picture others miss

• My weakness is sometimes waiting too long to act

Rating: ____/5

The Emotional Motivator (Kavita)

• I prioritize relationships and people's wellbeing

• I can sense emotional undercurrents in a room

• I struggle when I have to make decisions that hurt people

• People come to me when they need support

• My strength is building connection and loyalty

• My weakness is sometimes avoiding difficult accountability conversations

Rating: ____/5

The Political Player (Rajesh)

• I'm skilled at reading room dynamics and building alliances

• I think strategically about relationships and influence

• I'm comfortable in ambiguity and negotiation

• I know how to position information for maximum impact

• My strength is navigating complex organizational politics

• My weakness is sometimes crossing the line into manipulation

Rating: ____/5

The Fool Leader (Ramesh)

• I use humor to defuse tension and build rapport

• I'm uncomfortable with sustained seriousness or conflict

• People say I make difficult situations more bearable

• I sometimes use jokes to avoid dealing with hard truths

• My strength is maintaining morale and perspective

• My weakness is sometimes avoiding necessary difficult conversations

Rating: ____/5

The Decision Maker (Meera)

• I'm comfortable making difficult calls under pressure

• I take responsibility for outcomes, good or bad

• I sometimes carry too much weight alone

• People look to me in crisis situations

• My strength is clarity and decisiveness

• My weakness is sometimes not delegating enough

Rating: ____/5

The Destroyer (Vikram)

• I have high standards and enforce them consistently

• I'm direct, sometimes brutally so, about performance issues

• I believe accountability is more important than popularity

• People describe me as demanding or intimidating

• My strength is driving results and maintaining standards

• My weakness is sometimes damaging relationships in pursuit of outcomes

Rating: ____/5

The Challenger (Dev)

- I push for innovation and question established processes
- I get frustrated when others resist necessary change
- I believe strongly in my vision for improvement
- I'm willing to be unpopular if I think I'm right
- My strength is seeing possibilities others miss
- My weakness is sometimes alienating potential allies

Rating: ____/5

The Stressed Leader (Suresh)

- I feel constantly overwhelmed by competing demands
- I struggle to say no or delegate effectively
- I worry extensively about making mistakes
- I work long hours but still feel behind
- My strength is dedication and thoroughness
- My weakness is burnout and anxiety

Rating: ____/5

The Team Builder (Priya)

- I focus on helping others work together effectively
- I can see strengths in people others dismiss
- I get frustrated when people won't collaborate

• I believe the best outcomes come from collective effort

• My strength is facilitating and unifying diverse perspectives

• My weakness is sometimes overestimating willingness to cooperate

Rating: ____/5

Part 2: Deep Reflection Questions

• Which archetype did you score highest on? Does this align with how others perceive you?

• Which archetype did you score lowest on? What does this tell you about your blind spots?

• Think of your best leadership moment in the past year Which archetype were you embodying?

• Think of your worst leadership moment in the past year. Which archetype's weaknesses were showing?

Exploring Your Strengths:

• What do you do better than most leaders you know?

• When do people specifically seek you out? What does this tell you about your unique value?

• What aspect of leadership comes naturally to you without effort?

Confronting Your Weaknesses:

• What aspect of leadership consistently challenges you?

• What feedback do you receive repeatedly but struggle to address?

• What type of situation or person consistently triggers your worst leadership habits?

The Cost Question:

• What is your leadership style costing you personally? (Relationships, health, happiness, authenticity?)

• What is it costing your team? (Trust, performance, morale, innovation?)

• What is it costing your organization? (Results, culture, reputation, sustainability?)

Integration and Growth:

• Which archetype's strengths would most complement your natural style?

• If you could adopt one trait from an archetype different from yours, what would it be?

• What would "balanced leadership" look like for you specifically?

Situational Awareness:

• In what situations is your leadership style most effective?

• In what situations does it become a liability?

• How do you know when to lean into your natural style versus adapt?

The Relationship Reality:

• Who on your team complements your leadership style?

• Who clashes with it? Why?

• Are you building a team of people like you or people unlike you? Which do you need more?

The Transformation Question:

• If you could change one thing about your leadership starting tomorrow, what would it be?

• What's stopping you from making that change?

• What would success look like six months from now?

Part 3: Action Planning

Based on your reflections, complete the following:

My Primary Leadership Archetype:

____

My Secondary Archetype:

____

My Greatest Strength:

____

My Most Costly Weakness:

____

One Specific Behavior I Will Change:

____

How I Will Measure Progress:

____

Who Will Hold Me Accountable:

____

One Person I Need to Have an Honest Conversation With:

____

One Archetype's Strength I Will Develop:

____

My 30-Day Leadership Challenge:

____

APPENDIX B: THE NINE ARCHETYPES – A QUICK REFERENCE

The Calm Strategist (Arvind)

Core Drive: Understanding and pattern recognition

Greatest Strength: Sees connections and implications others miss; remains rational under pressure

Fatal Flaw: Analysis paralysis; waiting for perfect information that never comes

Trigger: Pressure to make decisions without adequate data

At Their Best: Provides critical analysis that prevents disasters; grounds decisions in evidence

At Their Worst: Observes dysfunction without acting; uses patience as excuse for avoidance

Needs From Others: Permission to act on 80% certainty; accountability for timely decisions

Leadership Lesson: Wisdom without action is just well-documented failure. Sometimes "good enough" is the only "perfect" you'll get.

Best Paired With: Decision Makers who force action; Challengers who push for progress

Worst Paired With: Other Strategists (nothing ever happens); Stressed Leaders (both stuck in overthinking)

Development Focus: Comfort with ambiguity; bias toward action; emotional intelligence

The Emotional Motivator (Kavita)

Core Drive: Human connection and care

Greatest Strength: Builds loyalty and trust; sees the person behind the position

Fatal Flaw: Avoiding difficult accountability conversations; empathy without boundaries

Trigger: Situations requiring "heartless" decisions; criticism framed as caring

At Their Best: Creates psychological safety; people feel valued and understood

At Their Worst: Enables poor performance; sacrifices results for feelings

Needs From Others: Support in having tough conversations; permission to enforce standards

Leadership Lesson: Caring about people includes caring enough to hold them accountable. Compassion without standards isn't kindness—it's abandonment.

Best Paired With: Destroyers who provide accountability balance; Decision Makers who make the hard calls

Worst Paired With: Other Motivators (no accountability); Stressed Leaders (mutual overwhelm)

Development Focus: Healthy boundaries; performance management; distinguishing support from enabling

The Political Player (Rajesh)

Core Drive: Influence and strategic positioning

Greatest Strength: Navigates complex organizational dynamics; builds coalitions

Fatal Flaw: Manipulation disguised as strategy; self-interest over collective good

Trigger: Loss of control or influence; being outmaneuvered

At Their Best: Connects people and resources; makes difficult negotiations work

At Their Worst: Creates distrust; plays people against each other for personal gain

Needs From Others: Accountability for transparency; challenging of hidden agendas

Leadership Lesson: Influence built on manipulation is fragile. True strategic thinking serves the mission, not just the strategist.

Best Paired With: Team Builders who channel politics toward unity; Calm Strategists who provide ethical framework

Worst Paired With: Other Political Players (endless manipulation); Destroyers (overt power vs. covert power clash)

Development Focus: Authentic relationship building; transparency; distinguishing strategy from self-interest

The Fool Leader (Ramesh)

Core Drive: Maintaining morale and deflecting heaviness

Greatest Strength: Makes difficult situations bearable; builds connection through humor

Fatal Flaw: Using jokes to avoid necessary discomfort; humor as shield

Trigger: Sustained seriousness; being asked to address pain directly

At Their Best: Keeps teams human during crisis; provides perspective and relief

At Their Worst: Undermines important conversations; prevents necessary processing of difficulty

Needs From Others: Permission to be serious; support in sitting with discomfort

Leadership Lesson: Humor can build people up or help them hide. Know which one you're doing in each moment.

Best Paired With: Destroyers who need humanizing; Calm Strategists who need lightness

Worst Paired With: Other Fool Leaders (nothing gets processed); Emotional Motivators (mutual avoidance)

Development Focus: Comfort with seriousness; emotional processing; using humor strategically rather than defensively

The Decision Maker (Meera)

Core Drive: Clarity and resolution

Greatest Strength: Makes difficult calls under pressure; takes ownership of outcomes

Fatal Flaw: Carrying too much alone; not delegating or trusting others

Trigger: Indecision or abdication in others; loss of control

At Their Best: Provides direction when everyone else is paralyzed; cuts through confusion

At Their Worst: Becomes bottleneck; prevents others' development; burns out from responsibility

Needs From Others: Support in delegation; accountability for letting go

Leadership Lesson: You can't be the only decider and also build a sustainable team. Teaching others to decide is more important than always deciding right.

Best Paired With: Calm Strategists who inform decisions; Team Builders who distribute ownership

Worst Paired With: Other Decision Makers (power struggles); Stressed Leaders (both carry too much)

Development Focus: Delegation skills; trust building; accepting imperfect decisions from others

The Destroyer (Vikram)

Core Drive: Standards and accountability

Greatest Strength: Drives results; maintains performance bars; doesn't accept excuses

Fatal Flaw: Confusing cruelty with toughness; breaking people in pursuit of outcomes

Trigger: Mediocrity; excuses; people who don't meet standards

At Their Best: Pushes teams to excellence they didn't know they could achieve

At Their Worst: Creates toxic environments; drives talent away; damages trust irreparably

Needs From Others: Feedback on impact; accountability for how outcomes are achieved

Leadership Lesson: You can have high standards without dehumanizing people. Accountability that destroys dignity ultimately destroys performance.

Best Paired With: Emotional Motivators who humanize the drive; Team Builders who repair relationships

Worst Paired With: Other Destroyers (mutual destruction); Challengers (both aggressively push, no support)

Development Focus: Empathy; distinguishing person from performance; building people up while maintaining standards

The Challenger (Dev)

Core Drive: Innovation and progress

Greatest Strength: Questions status quo; pushes for necessary change; sees future others miss

Fatal Flaw: Alienating allies; impatience with resistance; righteousness

Trigger: "We've always done it this way"; resistance to obvious improvements

At Their Best: Drives innovation; prevents stagnation; brings fresh perspectives

At Their Worst: Creates enemies; dismisses legitimate concerns; burns bridges

Needs From Others: Feedback on approach; help building coalitions; reality checks on timing

Leadership Lesson: Being right about the future doesn't matter if you can't bring anyone with you. Change management is as important as the change itself.

Best Paired With: Team Builders who help build coalitions; Calm Strategists who assess risks

Worst Paired With: Destroyers (both aggressively push); other Challengers (competing visions)

Development Focus: Stakeholder management; patience; framing change collaboratively

The Stressed Leader (Suresh)

Core Drive: Meeting all demands; avoiding failure

Greatest Strength: Dedication; thoroughness; commitment to excellence

Fatal Flaw: Burnout; inability to delegate; suffering in silence

Trigger: More demands with fewer resources; competing priorities; failure

At Their Best: Models dedication; catches details others miss; deeply reliable

At Their Worst: Becomes martyr; breaks down; models unsustainable patterns

Needs From Others: Permission to ask for help; support in boundary-setting; intervention

Leadership Lesson: You can't pour from an empty cup. Sustainability matters more than heroic suffering.

Best Paired With: Team Builders who distribute load; Decision Makers who take things off plate

Worst Paired With: Other Stressed Leaders (mutual drowning); Destroyers (more pressure)

Development Focus: Delegation; boundary-setting; self-care; asking for help

The Team Builder (Priya)

Core Drive: Unity and collective effectiveness

Greatest Strength: Facilitates collaboration; sees strengths in everyone; builds bridges

Fatal Flaw: Overestimating willingness to cooperate; exhaustion from constant facilitation

Trigger: People refusing to work together; fragmentation; wasted potential

At Their Best: Creates high-functioning teams; leverages diverse strengths; maintains unity

At Their Worst: Becomes peacekeeper instead of leader; avoids necessary conflict

Needs From Others: Appreciation of effort; support in accepting some people won't collaborate

Leadership Lesson: You can't want unity more than the team

does. Sometimes you have to let people fail together to learn to succeed together.

Best Paired With: Almost anyone (natural integrator); particularly Decision Makers and Calm Strategists

Worst Paired With: Highly resistant individuals who won't engage in collaboration

Development Focus: Accepting limitations of facilitation; knowing when to stop trying; self-care

APPENDIX C: GLOSSARY OF PHARMACEUTICAL MANUFACTURING TERMS

Key concepts for readers new to pharmaceutical production environments

Batch: A specific quantity of product produced in a single manufacturing cycle. Each batch is assigned a unique identifier for tracking and quality control purposes.

Batch Yield: The actual amount of product produced compared to the theoretical amount expected. Expressed as a percentage (e.g., 87% yield means 87% of expected output was achieved).

Contamination: Unwanted foreign material in a product that could compromise its quality, safety, or efficacy. Sources include microbial, chemical, or physical contaminants.

Cooling System: Equipment that regulates reactor temperature by removing excess heat generated during chemical reactions. Critical for preventing runaway reactions.

Distillation: A separation process that uses differences in boiling points to purify chemical compounds. Essential in pharmaceutical ingredient production.

Emergency Shutdown (ESD): Safety system designed to quickly bring equipment to a safe state when dangerous conditions are detected. Includes automatic and manual override mechanisms.

Feed Rate: The speed at which raw materials are introduced into a reactor. Precise control is critical for reaction quality and safety.

GMP (Good Manufacturing Practice): Regulatory standards ensuring pharmaceutical products are consistently produced and controlled according to quality standards. Violations can result in facility shutdowns.

HAZMAT (Hazardous Materials): Substances that pose risks to health, safety, or property. Pharmaceutical facilities handle various hazardous chemicals requiring special protocols.

Lakhs: Indian numbering unit equal to 100,000. Used throughout the book (e.g., ₹18 lakhs = ₹1,800,000 or approximately $21,600 USD).

Manual Override: Safety mechanism allowing operators to manually control equipment when automated systems fail. The physical lever or switch that enables this control.

Operator: Skilled technician responsible for running specific equipment (usually reactors) during production. Requires extensive training and certification.

Pharmaceutical Compound: Chemical substance used as an active or inactive ingredient in medicines. Apex produces compounds used in blood pressure medications.

Pressure Spike: Dangerous rapid increase in reactor pressure that can lead to equipment failure or explosion. Prevented through careful process control.

Production Efficiency: Metric measuring actual output against theoretical maximum capacity. Calculated as (actual output/maximum possible output) × 100.

Quality Check/QC: Testing and inspection processes ensuring products meet required specifications before release. Failed batches must be discarded.

Reactor: Large vessel where chemical reactions occur under controlled conditions. The core equipment in chemical manufacturing.

Reactor Hall: Facility section housing multiple reactors. Usually divided into zones (e.g., Reactor Hall A, B, C).

Regulatory Inspection: Government audit ensuring facility compliance with safety and quality standards. Failed inspections can result in production suspension.

Shift: Work period for operators and technicians. Most facilities run three 8-hour shifts to maintain 24/7 operations.

Solvent: Liquid substance used to dissolve or extract other materials during manufacturing. Many are flammable or toxic, requiring careful handling.

Standard Operating Procedure (SOP): Documented instructions for performing specific tasks consistently. Critical for quality and regulatory compliance.

Stress Fractures: Small cracks in metal equipment caused by repeated thermal cycling or pressure changes. Can lead to catastrophic failure if undetected.

Supervisor: Management role overseeing operators during a shift. Responsible for production, safety, and personnel management.

Temperature Protocol: Specified temperature ranges and adjustment procedures for each stage of a chemical process. Deviations can ruin batches.

Valve: Device controlling flow of materials through pipes. Can be manually operated or automated.

Valve Sequence: Specific order in which valves must be opened or closed during operations. Incorrect sequencing can cause safety hazards.

Common Measurements & Conversions:

Weight:

• Kilograms (kg) = 1,000 grams

• Lakhs/kg example: "847 kg output" = approximately 1,865 pounds

Volume:

• Liters (l) = 1,000 milliliters

• Common reactor capacity: 2,000-5,000 liters

Temperature:

• Celsius (°C) used throughout

• 42°C = 107.6°F (very hot working conditions)

• 215°C = 419°F (critical reactor failure temperature)

Currency:

• Rupees (₹) = Indian currency

• Lakhs (₹) = 100,000 rupees

• Crores (₹) = 10 million rupees

• Approximate conversion: ₹85 lakhs ≈ $102,000 USD (exchange rates vary)

Pressure:

• Measured in various units depending on context

• Pressure spikes, irregularities, and drops are all dangercus

Safety Color Coding:

Red: Emergency/danger - immediate action required Yellow: Caution/warning - attention needed Green: Normal operation - system functioning properly Blue: Information/mandatory action

Note: Pharmaceutical manufacturing is a highly regulated industry with extensive safety protocols. The terms and concepts in this glossary represent simplified versions for narrative purposes.